The Riddle of Consciousness

GOPI KRISHNA

Published by
The Central Institute for Kundalini Research
and The Kundalini Research Foundation, Ltd.

THE
RIDDLE
OF
CONSCIOUSNESS

CONTENTS

Editor's Note

Were this book to be taken from a time capsule and read a hundred years from now, what would the scientists and people say about it then? This question is appropriate because, in the truest sense, **The Riddle of Consciousness** is a book of revelation, and as such it calls for the judgment of time.

Although extremely rare, true Revelation has been a recurring phenomenon throughout history. Prophets from earliest times have appeared at intervals to forecast the end of an old order and the beginning of a new. A prophet was the legitimate mouthpiece of the gods. Divine utterances were conveyed to man through him. And, like Christ, Buddha and others, he served to guide the race through the most perilous of times. The prophet could see further into the future than other mortals and thus was able to warn of impending catastrophe when the people lost their way.

An instance of one kind of revelation is the Apocalypse, also known as the **Revelation of St. John the Divine.** But legions of scholars have puzzled over its meaning for centuries. John leaves the interpretation of his message up to us, but he does describe how it came to him: "I saw and beheld a door opened in heaven, and the first voice which I heard, a voice as a trumpet, speaking to me, one saying 'Come up hither,' and I will show thee the things that must come to pass hereafter."

Whether John's revelation is a carefully camouflaged metaphysical tract, a misinterpretation of ancient astronomical myths or a genuine prophecy, there still is no general

7

agreement. But that cannot be the case with **The Riddle of Consciousness**. It leaves no room for doubt or debate. Its message rings true as a bell. Though written in verse, it reads like simple prose. Anyone can grasp its meaning without difficulty.

What gives the prophet his ability to know what the future holds in store for mankind? The answer comprises one of the main themes of the book, for Gopi Krishna is a prophet and revealer both in the traditional as well as the modern sense. For example, he presents for the first time in the language of science the views expressed in the ancient Shaiva and Vedanta systems of philosophy of India. His ideas are just the opposite of what we are led to believe through our senses. Everything, including the Cosmos, is born of Consciousness, he says. Whatever knowledge man has gained of the physical world has all come out of consciousness and not from matter. It is this common delusion which **The Riddle of Consciousness** tries to demolish.

Gopi Krishna is giving us the cream of his message in this book, and it is in accordance with the fundamental teachings of all the revealed religions of the world. It is an inspiring and uplifting book, one with an interpretation on the phenomenon of existence that is truly amazing. According to it, the mystery of the universe is contained in the mystery of consciousness. The scientific exploration of matter is also an exploration of mind. For there is nothing beyond or above it.

This becomes apparent in the illuminated states of consciousness. In that state the knower and the known fuse into a Reality which is beyond expression. This wonder can only be experienced in Turiya or mystical ecstasy in which the present, past or future and the quarters of space coalesce into a marvellous Unity which is All.

8

PREFACE

I thank my friends whose labor, love and care
With me the genesis of this volume share;
A work which like a surging flood arose
Out of the depths of mind in rhyming prose;
An influx from the Void surrounding me,
Alive with consciousness we cannot see
With our corporeal eye, but can discern
When mind upon itself we know to turn.

The flaws in it which hurt the modern taste
I pray may not be judged in thoughtless haste,
To cavil but to run the Message down;
For language is the varying formal gown
Of thought, prone to change like a style of dress,
And since none of us can foresee or guess
What future preference or choice would be
It is unwise to adjudge this prophesy

Merely upon the ground of form or style
Which is in vogue now only for a while.

For certain cogent reasons I am led
To think that as I am not so well read,
And English is not my own mother tongue,
Nor did I practice penmanship when young,
Nor earlier than my forty-seventh year
Did I a single line indite or hear
Of this peculiar form of diction, nor
Had liking or a predilection for
This style, and so it took some years to attune
Myself to this gratuitous heavenly boon,
The reason why the writing takes this shape
And form, in which I ne'er wish it to drape,
Is that a clear, distinctive mark is used
So that the Message does not get confused
In loose strings of words which follow close
On one another in voluminous prose.

But of far more importance than the choice
Of language is the Message which this Voice
From the Void, using its own special kind
Of medium of expression through my mind,
Tries to deliver to apprise the race,
Absorbed in striving, at a frantic pace,
For power, supremacy and nuclear arms
Which now her growth and future glory harms,
That she is racing at full speed ahead
Towards a fast approaching night of dread.

How hard it is to express in rhyming prose
A theme, so abstract as this writing chose,
Can be assessed by penmen of our time
When they discuss philosophy in rhyme.
Since it does not conform to the routine
E'en those with faith in me are torn between
Their faith and doubts bred by the critic friends
Which may not end till what the book portends

Of future haps in due time comes to pass:
The clinching test of writings of this class.

Why not pay heed to what this Herald tells
About the future and the doom it spells
Of our rebellious ways of life, for long
Followed on principles entirely wrong,
With drastic changes in the coming years
In social, cultural and political spheres,
To breed a milieu for our healthy growth,
For sanity in thought and action both.

And if these hints with our own views accord,
Why should we not then, with faith in the Lord,
Make it the aim and object of our life,
Without withdrawing from our rightful strife,
To act in peaceful ways that tend to win
Its lost position for our soul within,
Firstly to attain our own divine rebirth,
And, secondly, to establish Truth on earth.

I know too well that, in this deafening din
And noise, I hardly can a hearing win:
A lone and feeble voice in the concourse
Of mighty super-powers girt with the force
Of nuclear arms, a gently whispered hint
Amid the roar of cannon and the glint
Of swords; a single drop of summer rain
Descending on a hot and arid plain,
Such should, to all appearance, be the fate
Of this prophetic utterance in this state
Of loud disorder, turmoil and uproar
Which gains all o'er in volume more and more.

But, strange to say, the Message with it brings
To me the visions of related things;
Of global wars and cataclysms to shake
Mankind out of her torpor soon to make
Her conscious of her glorious destiny,
Lost in the war of wits 'twixt you and me,

In gross obsession for the flesh and brawn,
In grandeur, glamour and the pleasures drawn
At the expense of soul, based on the blind,
Fallacious doctrines which deny to mind
Lasting existence, more pervasive than
The whole of cosmos we still fail to span.

I know despite the impossible handicaps,
Impassable hurdles and unbridgable gaps,
The Revelation shall achieve the aim
For which, in time, it as a Herald came;
And but a gesture at the appointed hour
To its foundations shake each mighty power,
Like giant trees uprooted by a storm,
Into a world-confederacy to form,
Changing the whole environment to leave
Man free the web of life afresh to weave.

And in less than two decades from this date
The world-conditions would assume a state
Of terror such that mortals on their knees
Would pray to Heaven the nightmare soon may cease.
This would be followed by a lightning war
With frightful devastation near and far;
A global conflagration that will make
A clean sweep of obstructions, roughly shake
Mankind out of her stupor and install
The rule of plenty, peace and joy for all,
After a spell of suffering so acute
That frozen with its horror one is mute.

Sarvodhya Enclave,
New Delhi, India.
Dated 7-3-1974.   Gopi Krishna

12

1

THE WONDER
THAT IS CONSCIOUSNESS

1

What I aver may seem to you, perhaps,
Blasphemous, unbelievable or odd,
For we are guilty of a common lapse,
When we forget that Consciousness is God;
When we ignore that what we see without
And our self inside, with no room for doubt,
Are diverse facets or, say, different shades
Of One Eternal Substance which pervades
The whole creation, everywhere the same
Beneath the varied dress of form and name.

All that we know: our learning, science, art
And all our universe of earths and suns
Are of a wondrous magic play a part,
Which change in consciousness makes clear at once,
When dumb with awe and wonder the ego sees
The world turned topsy turvy and the soul,

In one incredible moment of release,
From but a point become the Cosmic Whole.

From immemorial times we have deceived
Ourselves into the false belief that all
Impressions of the objective world received,
Which on the observing mind through senses fall,
Come from external objects and that we
Are transient shadows, born to live and die,
To come into being and then cease to be,
To act a while and then unmoving lie,
And that the Cosmic Ocean will not stop
Its movement for the loss of our one drop.

This most misleading and fallacious view
Has made mankind oblivious to a Truth
Which only can persuade her most to live
In peace and happiness and render smooth
Her path towards the Target she must win,
Which is: to find Divinity within.

Our consciousness is neither born nor dies
Nor after nascence does it e'er grow old,
Nor like a waif cast on the earth it tries,
A while, to enrich itself with power or gold,
But, on the contrary, this whole display,
This whole stir and this multitude of things
Emerge from it alone, like, let us say,
The lavish dream-scenario which all springs
From mind alone without external aid,
Appearing real for a while to fade.

It is not we who come into the world,
But, strange to say, the world is born in us
Before the day we in the womb lie curled,
And e'en before the birth of primary cells
We come into the orbit of a dream,
Dreamed by the Eternal Mind, or play a role
Assigned by a Cosmic Sun to a tiny beam
To act in Life's Drama as a soul.

Only a wrong assessment makes us doubt:
The world is inside us and not without,
And lost in this delusion mortal life
Becomes one long drawn night of ceaseless strife,
Of fear, contention, rivalry and hate,
Of passion and desire which ne'er abate,
But as decay sets in our earthly mould
With age, they gain on mind a firmer hold.

So our main effort oft becomes to gain
The highest profit from our brawn and brain,
To rise above our rivals in the field
In harvesting a more abundant yield,
To make the period of our stay on earth
A sunny day of comfort, ease and mirth:
At death to leave a fortune and a name
When, like a gambler who has lost the game,
We end in suffering e'er assailed by doubt
And e'er in woeful ignorance about
The Truth: that 'tis not Consciousness which dies
But the illusive veil before our eyes.

Not all the learned savants, now engaged
On consciousness-research, to ascertain
The plot and action of the drama staged
And how it is enacted by the brain,
Can e'er contrive in e'en a hundred years
To lift the veil this World-Enchanter wears.
This great exploit, to match with nature's plan,
Must be himself performed by every man.

To be alive, self-conscious and to know
That we exist to observe this baffling show
Is such a precious, such a most unique
Possession that no thinker, save one weak
In intellect and observation, can
Assign a secondary role to man
And not the primary, for this boundless Whole
Is but a veiled reflection of his soul,

Which Consciousness itself does build and plan
To see, perplexed, the Play as mortal man.

Where is the cosmos, what source lies behind
The hasty verdicts of the agnostic mind?
Wherefrom arise ideas, conceptions, views
And all the mass of learning, stories, news
With which the world is flooded in our day?
Whence comes what we believe or what we say?

And where is birth, where death and all our fears
That our temporal span is of some years?
Where are the sun, the moon, the wind and tide,
Those shining starry crowds which long abide?
Where are the wits and thinkers new or old,
Whence came the thought they did or now unfold?
And where is sorrow, sickness, suffering, pain
Or joy and cheer, love, beauty, loss or gain?
This is a point one ne'er can too much stress:
They all originate from consciousness!

Our image of the world, our personal views
And our experience come from that which lives,
Which knows, imagines, calculates and thinks,
And one observed fact with another links
To build the extremely complex world of thought
Which all exists, but where? We know it not.

Perhaps you hardly will believe me, when
I say what might shock nine men out of ten,
That this immense display, this Cosmic show
We carry all with us where'er we go!
The external world and our internal thought
Depend for their appearance on our mind.
What of them would survive if mind were not,
Can any one imagine, guess or find?
We are mistaken too when we concede
That subtler forms of matter form the base,
They too are products of the mind, indeed,
As, save it, who can their existence trace?

16

The argument that one, when fast asleep,
Does not observe the changes that are wrought
Round him, is shallow and does not go deep
Enough, for it again is wakeful thought
Which marks the changes and maintains the link
Between what one mind and the other think.
And even this point and counter-argument
Are but a mental product and event,
Because, save mind itself who can refute
That it of all existence is the root?

The talk about brain cells and genetic code
And all the carefully made-up bookish load
Is again an endless round of forms and names
Which suits the learned, who love wordy games,
For all whatever we know for sure or guess
Must e'er come from the spring of Consciousness.

E'en after a thousand years whate'er we know,
Whate'er we prove or still unproven show,
Shall not out of a different seed-bed grow,
But from the same mysterious spring-head flow.
Whate'er the future holds, whate'er is past
Nowhere save in the mould of mind is cast.

There is a twist in thinking here which needs
Correction, as it to grave error leads,
Matter on one, mind on the other side—
Who, of them, can between the two decide?
Save mind? And can you name a greater fool
Than one who, made to judge or bade to rule,
Would yield his chair or abdicate his throne
To those he judges—dead matter, earth and stone!

The source behind awareness, thought and will,
Desire, emotion, passion, logical skill,
Behind the world of knowledge, learning, wit,
Gathered with toil through ages, bit by bit,
Which, as supposed, does not exist in books,
But in the searching mind that in them looks,

To catch from man-made symbols what was said
By yet another mind, though long since dead,
Of worlds of past experience, form and name,
As flame is lit up by another flame.

Save mind there is no granary to store
What happens now or what transpired before,
The symbols used none else save it can read,
And like condensed material in a seed
That bears a tree, the invented symbols hold
Vast stores of knowledge but it can unfold.

Where then are our achievements highly praised,
The metropolises built, and mansions raised,
The amazing harvest of the industrial age
That has turned earth into a flood-lit stage?
And where the bloody wars and massacres
Which make us fear that we are growing worse?

Will not this knowledge also of our times,
Our great inventions, learning, wars and crimes,
Become known to our progeny at last
Through relics and the writings of the past?
To ponder often as we ponder now
Upon the achievements of our long since dead
Precursors, their ambition, hate and love
Which now exist nowhere save in our head.

The crowded streets with rich wares of our day
That make one giddy with the huge display,
Seen with eyes, known through pictures and accounts
Finally are products of our mental founts.
They too will soon become things of the past
Effaced, save when in future eyes are cast
On documents and remnants which survive
To keep our actions and exploits alive.

Whate'er exists or happens in the world,
Whoe'er arrives or out of it is hurled,

18

Analyzed lastly will be traced to mind
In league with something which we cannot find,
By which this vast creation comes into view,
To pass, with marching time, from old to new,
And hence all we experience, know and see
Is but an image, not reality.

Our modern scholars try to find without
What is within, beyond a shade of doubt.
The ponderous cosmos which they see before
Their eyes, when fast asleep is there no more,
And reappears, with change, when one awakes,
Which Cosmic-mind in this duration makes.

When one is dead it is not soul has died
And left the physical world which he espied
Before, but that his image in our mind
Has ceased and save in thought we no more find,
Because the world-creative Pranic link
That made his shadow-body act and think,
In his and our identical mental world,
Is broke, and off the image has been hurled.

We strut and dance upon the imaginary stage
Of mind where lust, desire and passion rage,
Clothed in the fancied dress of flesh and bone,
Of phantom earth of water, air and stone,
All but creations of a magic base
Which, as the mind and matter it can trace,
Is all: the actor, action and the stage,
The rogue, the hero, the knight and his page,
The rabble and the elite, the saint and fraud,
This infinite creation and its Lord!

2

This vast amphitheatre, the earth and sky
Remember ne'er is seen with carnal eye
For nothing born of what is lifeless, dead
Can hold such vastness, to such distance spread,

Nor e'en when chemistry reshapes its forms,
Can it evince desire or harbour storms
Of passion, breed ambition, grief or joy,
In changing phases, or enraptured toy
With the dear cantours of a fair beloved,
With senses ravished and heart deeply moved.

Nothing born of the earth, on which we tread,
Not e'en the earth itself, to feeling dead,
With all her vast expanse has space to hold
The enormous world we with our mind enfold.

Naught is so laughable and tragic both
That some men should ascribe their birth and growth
To lifeless elements they see, hear or smell,
And thus by their erroneous thinking spell
The doom of their instinctive wish to find
The truth behind the enigma of their mind.
Because once they the faulty premise grant
Then but to assemble all the learned cant
To prove it, oft consumes their buoyant youth
And robust prime to turn away from truth!

Some there are who concede that mind is born
Not out of matter but the two are one,
And that by some unknown alchemy both
Have come together in organic growth,
And save in living bodies mind has no
Distinct existence, so death ends the show.

This means they too conceive organic life
To be a part of nature's aimless strife,
With no design to fashion rational man
And other creatures on a definite plan.

By what mischance has it then come about
That nigh in all spheres of life without
A well-considered and well-thought-out plan
A slipshod action ne'er appeals to man?

Why should the urge to have a goal or aim
Then sway the whole life of this thinking flame?
Then why the higher forms of life, when born,
And e'en the lower ones, like flowers or corn,
Conform to a definite pattern when they grow,
And from the first regard to order show?

Incredible though it seems, it is a fact
That Prana and pure consciousness react
On one another to produce the myth
Of this stupendous world we battle with.

Still more incredible is the further fact
That with restraint of passions, righteous act,
Devotion, fellow-feeling, mental calm
And thought sublime, which all act like a balm,
Prana in faint degrees works out a change
And, much enhanced in power, brings in its range
Of observation new domains of life,
As different from this world of stress and strife
As sky is from the earth, sunshine from gloom,
Or as from winter is the spring in bloom.

Then consciousness a wondrous aspect wears,
So lofty and sublime that all our fears
And doubts about ourselves dissolve at once,
As if illumined by a hundred suns
Of knowledge to be assured the Vision seen
Is That which will be, is and e'er has been;
The Source Eternal of all that is known—
The world—of that too by which it is shown—
The mind—and process by which this is done:
The whole scheme of creation in but One.

In this amazing, radiant Presence all
The staggering worlds, which awe us and enthrall,
Become a ghostly shadow seen at night;
A far-off melting cloud in sunshine bright,
While mind, with ego vastly whittled down,
In mute astonishment sees itself drown

Into one all-enfolding Life sublime,
Only pure consciousness, devoid of time
And space, One all-embracing world of love
And joy not found on earth or heaven above.

Why scholars find it hard to reconcile
What I say with their bulky fossil file,
With all the enormous odds life had to face
At last to blossom as the human race,
With all the inhuman struggle, bloody strife,
Which marked the birth of every form of life,
With all the frightful happenings there have been
Since life's appearance on the earthly scene,
Is that the grim account does not accord
With our conceptions of a gracious Lord.

But ere they voiced their condemnation did
A single skeptic find out what is hid
Below the surface layer of his mind,
And, if so, in this drive what did he find?
If not, how can we draw conclusions when
We have but half the world before our ken—
The physical world observable with the mind—
But not a whit about what lies behind
The mind, of what mysterious stuff is made
The observer, always acting in the shade;
Hence in this enterprise how can we win,
When we know nothing of the world within?

The story of Life shall be writ again
Just when we solve the riddle of the brain
And know more of the doleful tale of woe
To which, they say, we our existence owe.
And if not we, our progeny shall see
How many different versions there will be
Before the cipher of the brain is read
To melt full many phantoms we have bred.

The giant reptiles, many a bird and beast,
Which all have vanished, leaving not the least

Sign, showing why they rose to fall a prey
To extinction after a sorry, fruitless stay,
To eat their bellies full, to sleep and lust
And then inexplicably come to dust.

And why? Because the drama Life displays
On earth, commencing from her earliest days,
Is not a separate show but only a part
Of a colossal one, which did not start
From earth, but acting everywhere in space,
Upon the unbounded stage of time and place,
Performs one act here and another there,
All planned and thought out with consummate care,
Showing immortal life in countless roles,
As countless as the starry host which strolls
In the sky, leisurely to mortal eyes,
But with terrific speed which thought defies.

Once when the lamp of this Research is lit,
Then the whole armoury of mortal wit
Will not be only used to assess the speeds
Of stars and planets, but to observe the seeds
Of life which, spread on every inch of space,
Require a more observant eye to trace
Their hid existence e'en in globes of fire,
For they abode the expanse of space entire.

Most of us have faint glimpses in our dreams
Of our identity with cosmic streams
Of life, though rarely, when our soul awakes
To its forgot divine estate and makes
A fleeting visit to its native home,
Unhampered by flesh in the void to roam.

This gives the impression of a flying leap
Or bulkless flight to ego in the sleep,
And in the process oft with fear awakes,
As such a bodiless flight or jumping shakes
Its instinct, and so brings it back again
To normal, with the tether of the brain!

In our extensive travels during dream
Some of the experiences impossible seem.
They are so, when from earthly angle seen,
But not when they depict a cosmic scene,
Nor when they re-enact a former role
Or play a future one, because the soul
Has its abode in one Eternal Whole,
With one, once for e'er writ, immutable scroll
Of Fate, in which what is or has occurred,
Or shall occur exists now word for word.

And so where'er in space one acts a part
Or shall act or has acted from the start
The soul can dimly glimpse it, whether past
Or future, with cheer, sorrow or aghast.

But oft, securely bound with ego's chain
It thinks itself to be the actor main,
And so in dreams it hovers in between
The dreaming ego and the cosmic scene
And in confusion mixes up the two,
Wondering how it could e'er such actions do,
Pressures of flesh and mind, desire, pride, lust
Their presence always in these tableaux thrust,
Rendering the scene confusing in the extreme
Which makes it hard to read aright a dream.

Since these peeps at the past or future are
Distorted by the sense-lined corridor
Of brain, the muddled dream-scenes often wear
A weird appearance, so strange and queer,
That from times immemorial they have been
A standing riddle for the wise and keen.

This is how Brihadaranyaka Upanishad
describes the state of soul in sleep:—
"When one goes to sleep he takes along[1]
the material of this all-containing world,

---

[1]Brihadaranyaka Upanishad 4.3.9-14 translated by R.E.Hume.

24

himself tears it apart, himself builds it up,
and dreams by his own brightness,
by his own light. Then his person becomes
self-illuminated.

There are no chariots there, no spans no roads.
But he projects from himself chariots, spans, roads.
There are no blisses there, no pleasures, no delights.
But he projects from himself blisses, pleasures, delights.
There are no tanks there, no lotus-pools, no streams.
But he projects from himself tanks, lotus-pools, streams.
For he is a creator.

On this point there are the following verses:

"Striking down in sleep what is bodily,
Sleepless he looks down upon the sleeping (senses),
Having taken to himself light, there returns to his place
The golden person, the one spirit.

Guarding his low nest with the breath,
The Immortal goes forth out of the nest.
He goes where'er he pleases—the Immortal,
The golden person, the one spirit.

In the state of sleep going aloft and alow,
A god, he makes many forms for himself—
Now, as it were, enjoying pleasure with women,
Now, as it were, laughing, and even beholding fearful sights.

People see his pleasure ground;
Him no one sees at all."

Now some people say: "That is just his waking state,
for whatever things he sees when awake,
Those too he sees when asleep." (This is not so, for)
there (i.e. in sleep) the person is self-illuminated.

This from Rumi:
"The mystics in their dream of transport close
their eyes but still they earth and heaven behold."

A blooming centre opens in the brain;
A light begins to burn amid a rain
Of nectar, watering deep with bliss untold
A new awareness in which we behold
The world or, when asleep, the realm of dreams,
As if enveloped in refulgent beams
Of living splendour out of which arise
Realities or dream-scenes one espies,
When waking or asleep, in either case
The varied forms of one eternal base.

Remember that the place where you now stand
Fully awake, on water, air or land,
Can be the haunt of many other kinds
Of life, with different bodies, senses, minds
Made of a finer stuff than what we see
In dreams, impossible though it seems to be.

The mystery of life does not unfold
Its inconceivable depth till we behold
The world afresh with transcendental sight,
Which only our misjudgments can set right,
And make the scholars conscious of their faults;
For we live shut from light in buried vaults.

Whether one is asleep or wide awake,
Whether the world seems real or but fake,
Both in the dreaming state and wakefulness
Whate'er is seen stems from consciousness;
Both different planes of one creative spring,
One bound, the other with a looser string.

The enlightened miss not in the state of dream
The glory that surrounds the effulgent beam
Of life in them—their now awakened soul—
And as the multiple dream-scenes unroll
Before their view, they always have in sight
The golden halo making all things bright
And sunny, for now the beholder wears
The aureate crown sung of by Vedic seers.

The Atman circled by a sheath of gold
Illumines all whate'er it does behold,
Awake or dreaming, bathing in its light
In front, behind or to the left or right
All that it comes across; a floating orb
Of golden sentience still clad in the garb
Of flesh, residing on earth, but afloat
In astral spheres, from mortal thought remote.

The dream experience some of us believe
Is born of day, and we re-spin and weave
What we long for or suffer during day,
Which all comes masquerading in the play
Of sleep, requiring oft a psychiatrist
The tangled skein of these scenes to untwist.

Floundering in the streams of modern thought
We seldom stop to ponder, as we ought
To do, that when we undeniably find
Wisdom behind our body and our mind:
Behind the sentience which controls our growth
From the embryonic stage and childhood both;
Which smoothly runs, unnoticed and unseen,
Our body—the most marvellous machine
On earth—about which we are still in dark,
And still some of its wonders fail to mark;
Which is behind the knowledge we display;
And keeps it stored in a mysterious way:
In short, the wisdom but to which we owe
Our life, our mind and flesh and all we know.
Can you suppose this gracious Wisdom turns
Into a Satan when the night-lamp burns,
Acting in such perverse ways in our dream
Which when awake to us abhorrent seem?
Or is there something wrong in current thought
Which e'en in realms divine is spreading rot!

"It matters not" Says Nanak,
"how many cart-loads of learning you have[1]

---

[1]Hymns of Guru Nanak, translated by Khushwant Singh.

27

nor what learned company you keep;
it matters not how many boat-loads of books
you carry or the quantity of knowledge
with which you manure your tree of knowledge;
it matters not how many years and months
you spend in study nor with what passion
and single-mindedness you pursue knowledge.
Only one thing really matters, the rest
is but whirwind of the ego. . . . There are
a hundred falsehoods but this one sovereign truth—
that unless truth enters the soul
all service and study is false."

It is time when the learned who have shut
Their thinking in the old, out-moded rut,
And still ascribe mind to capricious chance,
Or latest to the mere fortuitous dance
Of D.N.A. or some such molecules,
Should now more wisely scan the rigid rules
Of life and frame a judgment, if they can,
That if mind is a product of sheer chance
To what do they ascribe their own advance?
From what then, if there is no wider source
Of knowledge, do they new discoveries force?

The plea: Man has a most productive brain,
With vast reserves which normally remain
Unused, and in some cases come into play.
In genius or some wonder of the day,
Is as fallacious as it is inane.
For now the point arises what made the brain
Of man with, as they urge, fortuitous skill
To evince, what matter lacks, design and will
Which can dig out from mind's still brimful mine
New gems, no one can name yet or define.

3

Let not the thought that millions, all like you,
Reflect the light of mind, as drops of dew

In countless mini-forms reflect the sun,
And of this multitude you are but one:
Let also not the thought that countless dead,
Since man arose on earth, when once the thread
Of life was broken, ne'er again returned
To visit former scenes, where they had burned
With love and hate, again to ignite the fire
Which ne'er rekindles once it does expire,
Depress or pain you, for you ne'er e'en once
Were born or died, nor had a sire nor sons.
Unborn, eternal, your Self is the cream
Of all creation, now lost in a dream.

Let not the thought that you are not endowed
With beauty, strength or wit, that make one proud,
Nor are pre-eminent nor have wealth nor name,
Nor gift nor knowledge nor can light the flame
Of love, disturb your mind for there is naught
On earth which you lack now or e'er had not.
You are the Spring-head, though you know not it,
Of all the riches, talent, charm and wit.

The need is to o'er-haul the organic chain
That binds the soul to a yet imperfect brain,
When all the gifts and charms which fill your dreams
Shall shine in you as on the sun shine beams
Of light: a kingdom which is yours, in fact,
Attained with noble conduct, thought and act.

Reverses, sickness, suffering, pain and grief,
All transient shadows that attend your brief
Stay in the dream-land of this monstrous world,
In time out of your pathway shall be hurled,
When diligently you pull yourself awake
And free your mind of this bewitchment shake.

Slowly when Cosmic laws—parts of this dream—
Become known more and more the imprisoned beam
Of God's own Splendour which, in truth, you are
Shall find new ways to end grief, pain and war,

And, though still clothed in flesh, shall live awake
To its primordial glory, soon to make
The earth an Eden and its time of stay
Of beauty, love and joy one long-drawn day.

It is a staggering truth more staggering than
The cosmos with all its colossal span,
That the invisible flame of sentience we
Possess can house the universe we see,
With time and distance, and its crowds of suns
And earths, whose number into trillions runs,
Some visible, others hidden from our eye,
Of such enormous size they thought defy.
But with all its intelligence no beast can
An inkling have of things revealed to man
Whene'er he contemplates the twinkling orbs
And in their mystery his mind absorbs.

This feeling is not present in the beast
Although its sense equipment is, at least,
As strong and as effective as in man,
But e'en so its awareness fails to scan,
Deduce and measure the time-span and size
Of the world and in this the difference lies.

Nor by instruction or by training can
We teach an animal to think like man.
Hence our idea of vastness of the size
Of the universe or its duration lies
Not so much in what is perceived by us
As in the quality of Consciousness!

The world goes suddenly wrong for the insane
Who starts to hear and see with the same brain
What for the rest is mere trash and refuse,
Creations of a fancy running loose,
A sudden breakage of the rational chain,
Leaving imagination with no rein.

But if we e'en this issue weigh a bit
In all its bearings we shall have to admit

That his mad state is yet another phase
Of consciousness, when with his eyes ablaze
With anger, sad with grief or wild with fright
He talks, gesticulates or rushes to fight,
Conveying by these signs the change wrought,
Real or fancied, in his mind and thought,
Not in his senses which still serve more or less,
But in the hid depths of his consciousness.

Where now the cosmos with its awful size
And vast duration, which confounds the wise?
Where now the magic of the sky at night,
Although the starry worlds are still in sight?
And where the wonder of this whole display?
For that delirious mind in disarray?

If we now study the mind of a child,
A suckling babe, when with eyes opened wide
It looks with wonder at the star-lit sky,
And pointing up e'en gives a joyous cry.
Does it have e'en the least idea of what
Interpretation we on the show put?

And does it realize each twinkling star
Has such a prodigious mass or is so far?
Or does it know aught of the mysteries
Which crowd in what the astronomer now sees?
Perhaps to grow in future wiser still
And realize, like grown ups, with a thrill
That there are wonders still, he failed to see,
Which shed a new light on the mystery.

Why take an infant, take a normal man
Refined in taste, who dwells when e'er he can,
On things sublime: the mystery of life
And death, weighs all the ideas and theories rife;
The problem of Eternity and soul
With their relation to the Cosmic Whole,
And sunk in reverie deep in his mind,
When all absorbed, a nameless joy can find.

Suppose a sudden sorrow makes him sad
Reverses depress, a loss makes him feel bad,
A shock unnerves, injustice causes a smart
Bad news dismays or treachery cuts at heart,
Or some fear or anxiety weighs him down
Be he a millionaire or one wearing a crown,
The days grow gloomy, sleepless pass the nights,
No games amuse, no words cheer, naught delights
Divine recedes, sublime, grown distant, fades,
Only anxiety, grief or fear pervades
The mind which only a little while before
Had been so gay, so hearty to the core.

No more that joy in books, no more those themes
That had consoled him with alluring dreams,
And in the desert of life acted the role
Of an oasis for his thirsty soul,
Despond now chokes the genial flow of life
And makes him cross with children and his wife.
The same refined and cultured mind that had
Been so congenial acts now like one mad.

Hopeless depression so completely holds
His mind in its grip e'en when night unfolds
The glory of the star-filled firmament,
That the dark mood does not the least relent
With what had erstwhile been his great delight
To gaze long at the glowing sky at night!

Distraction, worry, grief, exceeding stress
Have such a marked effect on consciousness,
They change behaviour, habit, taste and mood,
Kill appetite, create distaste for food,
Deprive of pleasure, hobby, study, sport
And one's whole personality distort
For some time, till the mind recovers back
The equilibrium shattered by the attack.

In all such cases when someone is torn
With worry, fear, anxiety or is worn

With sorrow, suffering or care he is prone
To be affected to the flesh and bone,
To find himself beset by fright and gloom
In e'en a palace lush with flowers in bloom.

The sky looks overcast, earth alive with threats,
And life a bed of thorns, which galls and frets,
Calmness and cheer become things of the past,
As if a heavy blanket has been cast
Upon the mind, to snuff the heartening light
Of peace and joy and change to gloomy night.

So with the action of emotions raised
By worry, grief or fear one can be crazed,
Made anxious, sad, depressed, morose, afraid
And these conditions at once do not fade,
But cause affliction for a varying spell
Of time, which may match in severity hell.

These actions and reactions of our mind,
Caused by emotions, often do not find
Us eager to discover the reason why
We cannot over-come them, if we try,
And what is more regrettable we do not
To this important issue give our thought
That if anxiety or shock, grief or fear
In such alarming way our mind can sear;
Make it acutely anxious, gloomy, sad
Distressed, distracted, tense, distraught or mad,
Cannot the unnatural ways of life we lead,
Our trifling with the right in thought and deed,
Create the same conditions, faint but sure,
Which too our Pranic Spectrum make impure
To cause the turmoil and uproar we see
Today, with no clue to the mystery.

This is the vicious harvest of our fault
When matter over mind we chose to exalt,
Assigning mind the office of a maid
For serving Soma to be highly paid,

And those this office diligently filled,
Alas! the incentive to self-knowledge killed,
Leaving uprooted mankind in a lurch,
Wavering between its Soma and the church.

4

It rests with us, the dreamers of the dream,
To lie oblivious, till the sentient beam
Of life departs to leave the mortal coil
And cold to mingle with the soil,
Or wake up to the Truth, while dreaming still,
To infuse in our emotion, thought and will
The knowledge of our true Divine Estate,
And live up to that knowledge until Fate
Comes at the appointed hour to burn the Light,
And leave us dazzled by the glorious sight.

What irrepairable loss do we sustain,
When dead to Forces active in the brain,
We live awareless of the target aimed
And, with the mind and senses still untamed,
By o'er attention to the carnal side
More firmly in the dream condition bide?

Still more the loss, when we securely bind
Into our ways of thought the plastic mind
Of children, innocent until we din
Into their ears the charm that they should win
Success in all whate'er they undertake,
And in this effort spare no pains to make
Temporal plenitude their primary goal,
With hardly a word to tell them that the soul
Demands their first attention, as it should,
To make them, more than rich or powerful, good.

We can be certain that the child will learn
What we have learnt and shall teach him in turn

To instill the knowledge we have so far gained
And make his thinking, like our own, when trained.

With all this knowledge at his beck and call
He may add something more, beyond it all,
Born of his observation, thought and skill
Or e'en intuition, last a riddle still.
In each case his addition, more or less,
Is all an offering from his consciousness.
So we see lastly what he learns or finds
Comes from his own or from his elders' minds!

The same has happened from the farthest past,
One mind has taught another, first to last,
And this accumulated knowledge, oft
We call ours, not that it comes from aloft,
A racial store, deposited bit by bit
By consciousness through those she gifted it.

We seldom realize how much we owe
To our upbringing, for all that we know,
Or have in mind today, in every sphere
Of knowledge, was collected here and there,
From prehistoric times ere man began
To think and in a rational way to scan.

Thus every bit of wisdom, every shred
Of knowledge, every fact about the world
Have all been contributed in small amounts
By consciousness from her own varied founts.

The glory and the wonder of our life
But seldom strikes us, since it is so rife
And common, that we rarely stop to think
That our awareness is the only link
Between us and the unmeasured Cosmic mass,
Our thoughts and fancies through the mind which pass,
With our ideals, ambitions, goals and aims
Our interests, hobbies, studies, sports and games,
Our talents, business, urges and desires
To vanish suddenly when life expires.

Our wrong appraisal of life has consigned
To the back-yard the wonder of the mind,
Our lone means to know and appreciate
The great advance in knowledge up-to-date,
What scientists and scholars have to say
About their contributions day to day,
To inform, instruct, intrigue, excite or thrill,
Yet with no word about awareness still,
Though what they say and what we hear from them
All stems from consciousness, the only gem
Which sheds the light that helps us know and see
Our-selves, the cosmos and their mystery!

Why are you worried that our life is short,
That suffering and disease can mind distort,
Reduce it all to such a sorry state
It fails to reason and evaluate,
While all the world continues as before,
Concernless whether there is one mind more
Or less or whether one has fallen ill
Or died, for there are myriads living still,
And millions each year pass beyond the bourne
Whence none returns to extend the past sojourn.

Whether a mind is ailing or insane,
Or thinking rightly with a normal brain,
It is the one source of our knowing all
That to the world or to us does befall.

That minds are crooked or cracked, insane or sound,
Or whimsical or sickly is no ground
To assume that it is not the primal cause
Of all creation and its rigid laws,
Because the very fact that we define
One mind as sound and one ill is a sign
That it possesses a firm unvarying base
Which variations in its state can trace.

The flaw in our contention lies in this
That, when discussing mind, we often miss

To pay attention to the weighty fact
That whether healthy or ill, sane or cracked,
It is not the individual mind that lies
Behind the world we live in, vast in size,
But its primordial Source, the Oceanic Base
Of which a drop lives in the human race,
And all the numberless terrestrial forms,
Of life, abiding everywhere in swarms.

How can it, in the least, affect the sun
If its effulgent rays fall, one by one,
To light up once a horse and then a cow
Another time a crow and soon a sow,
A lunatic, a genius or a crank,
A stream full of fish or a sandy bank,
Our point is that awareness is the sun
Whose rays light up the world and make it run.

The issue here arises is there ought
Besides awareness, with its mind and thought,
On which its lustre shines to bring to light
What else would buried lie in endless night.
In other words, is there a physical stuff
Which needs awareness but to light it up,
If so, the cosmos is then real too,
And consciousness spectator of the view?

The notion that ought can exist besides
Awareness in our wrong deduction bides.
How can the knower come to know the known
Unless a bond between the two has grown.
Unless there is a third to act the part
Of bringing them together with his aıt,
To serve the purpose of a link between
The abstract seer and the material seen;
And this third partner, too, must have a fourth
To lodge him nicely in between them both,
Also, perhaps a fifth to make it sure
That for some time the union does endure.

The scholars who consider mind and flesh
As an inseparable compound, afresh
Raise issues human thought can never solve,
If it does for a thousand years evolve.
For how can things dissimilar at the base
Completely merge the plan of life to trace,
Needing such harmony between the two
That 'tis impossible to determine who
Is the author, flesh or mind, for as we find
Some men hold matter basic and some mind.

If we hold matter as the cause of life,
And for some time this theory has been rife,
Then it too must have consciousness diffused,
At its own basic levels, which was used
To build up more and more elaborate forms
Of life, by chance, amid tempestuous storms,
Antarctic rigour and extremes of heat
Until in man it gained a lofty seat.

But here again we come across a knot,
For it does not appeal to rational thought,
That one can be alive and dead at once,
Or half-alive and half-dead, and have sons
And daughters, all by chance, born of a stone,
Or half-dead rock, turned into flesh and bone:
A most preposterous theory in which mind
Has no place in the genesis of mankind.
And only lifeless, aimless forces spin
And weave the fabric which in man, could win
To such an intellectual height that he
Believes a greater height there ne'er can be.

How rudimentary sentience could contrive
With keen intelligence to live and thrive,
To exact obedience from the very start
From matter down to its minutest part,
And build a complex structure, like the brain
Of mammals, strictly with a casual chain,

Unless there is complete accord between
The two, and both are now and e'er have been
Two faces of but one substance, so remote
From us that we its wonder fail to note.

These fitful speculations of our mind
The answer to the Riddle ne'er can find,
If we continue for eternity
Into this mystery to fit a key,
For mortal wit and reason constitute
One single facet of an Absolute,
Who, all pervading, acts in countless spheres
And in each one a different costume wears,
Out of which man's intelligence is but one,
One single weak beam of a blazing sun.

One ray of millions which light other globes,
Wearing a million kinds of formal robes,
Each with its own awareness which, distinct
From others, differently can know and think.
In short, the cosmos is a teeming crowd
With varied types of consciousness endowed.

It is no wonder we treat as a myth
Ethereal worlds beyond perception with
Our sense equipment, so extremely poor
That to this day we could not make it sure
What matter is and from what stuff arise
The nebular formations on the skies?
What force is gravity, what time and space
Or whence come comets in the void to race?
And hence but little credence might be lent
To what I say that our whole life is spent
In chasing shadows, while round us abides
An ocean of awareness on all sides
But since it is so subtle we are hurled
Into error for 'tis a different world.

5

We value less what we should value more—
Our soul—because the world is e'er before
Our eyes, so we forget the observer who
Brings all that we perceive into our view.
Thus too fond of the outer passing show
We are indifferent to what we should know,
What is far more important for our weal
Than all the external goods with which we deal,
That far more rare and precious than the whole
Of earth is our rich kingdom of the soul.

But this ennobling thought we oft ignore
In our anxiety to reach before
The rest whate'er of value we can find,
Which leaves us little time to explore the mind
To unearth that one unvalued treasure chest
Of all the goods of earth which is the best.

What all the great religions sought to teach,
What Buddha, Christ and Vyasa came to preach,
What Plato, Shankra, Rumi and the rest
Of great religious thinkers tried their best
To expound with all the force at their command,
And in the richest language of their land,
In different tones proclaims the mighty Truth,
The one and only Gospel that can soothe
The fever of our mind that of this whole
Boundless display the Centre is the soul.

What can the study of a thousand books
Avail, if goods of earth, like smiling crooks,
Entice our mind and keep it from the quest
That only can unco'er the Royal Crest
Of Life Eternal which, ordained to crown
The search of man for Truth, on reaching down
Into the unfathomed depth of his own soul,
Shows God in him and He in God, the goal
Of all religious practice rightly done
To make soul and the world fuse into One.

The famous maxims of the Enlightened seers
Of Upanishads which their devout compeers
Preserved to last full many thousand years,
During which empires sank in blood and tears,
That "My Atma and Brahma are but one,"
That "Thou art That" and "All this is Brahman"
Which have resounded through vast centuries
To set full many a restless mind at ease,
Admit no other meaning save this one:
That soul is one with Life's Eternal Sun
From which both creatures and the worlds are born,
Like light-beams shed by but one sun at morn.

Millions acknowledge and revere the truth
Of this immortal teaching, but, in sooth,
They often fail to spell out what it means:
That all experience of the external scenes,
Of mammoth cosmic hosts or time and space
Is but an out-growth of a solid base,
A vast projection of the immortal soul,
The visible peak of an invisible Whole,
The myriad branches of a buried root,
Or of the one and only Absolute,
And "Thou art That" O, yon unheeding soul,
Lost to thy Kingdom in an illusive role.

The real aim of all religious search,
Of worship in a temple, mosque or church,
Is not to win to something from us far,
Or inaccessible, like a shooting star,
But just to turn within the wayward mind,
Its sensual chains to loosen and unbind,
So that free of the prison we have built
For it ourselves, unconscious of the guilt,
It gains the freedom, we to it deny,
To gaze amazed with its celestial eye,
At its divine proportions far from aught,
That can be e'er conceived by human thought.

How can we claim to know our faith aright
When we miss what the Founders had in sight,

To find the glorious empire of the soul
And, all oblivious to this, make it roll
In dust in hot pursuit of earthly goods,
Which loom large e'en in introspective moods
By which, free of the carnal, it could win
To its dominion it must seek within,
Not outside, for what it perceives without
Is its own masked reflection spread about.

"My Guru," Lalla[1] sings, "Said but one word,
Turn from the outer to the inner world,
This word I made my only aim and stance,
And with abandon thence began to dance."
"Water" she adds at yet another place,
"When frozen with cold turns to ice and snow,
Three forms assumed but by one single base,
Which melt again and one formation show,
When the sun shining greater warmth brings,
So when the Sun of Consciousness ascends
This world of sentient and insentient things,
With all that makes up this creation ends,
To merge into One from which All springs."

This is how Dante[2] tries to express the same
Experience of the Universal Flame,
The One devoid of any shape or form
Become the giant world of calm and storm,
The all-pervading, ineffable Light
Which mirrored as creation meets our sight:

"O grace abounding, whereby I presumed
So deep the eternal light to search and sound
That my whole vision was therein consumed!

In that abyss I saw how love held bound
Into one volume all the leaves whose flight
Is scattered through the universe around;

---

[1] Lalla's sayings see Lal Ded by Jaya Lal Kaul.
[2] Dante—The Divine Comedy, translated by Barbara Reynolds.

42

How substance, accident and mode unite
Fused, so to speak, together, in such wise
That this I tell of it is simple light.

Yea, of this complex I believe mine eyes
Beheld the Universal Form—in me,
Even as I speak, I feel such joy arise."

"From all eternity the beloved unveiled"
Says Jami[1] "In the loneness of the Unseen,
His beauty held the mirror to his face
And to himself his loveliness displayed,
As the Spectator and the Spectacle,
No eyes but his surveyed the universe,
And all was one with no duality,
With not the least pretense of 'mine' or 'thine'."

When you their poetry detachedly con
What other meaning can you put upon
The words of Dante and the Sufi saints,
Despite their chosen faith and its restraints,
When they say God-head and the soul are one,
The world a veiled appearance of the Sun
Of Life—all three essentially the same—
Though different outwardly in form and name?
What other sense can these plain words convey
Save that soul of God's Splendour is a Ray.

When Christ said: "I and Father are but one,
I live in these men and He lives in me,"
Does it not mean the Father and the Son
And all the world of life, the basic three,
Are in reality one and the same;
The sparks that fly from One Eternal Flame
Which, as the universe, the soul and God,
Is immanent in us here and abroad.

---

[1]Jami—translated by R.A. Nicholson.

When modern mystics, speaking from their heart,
Aver that they and God are not apart,
But one and that they share the Light Divine
Which all the objects of the world enshrine,
They voice the same immortal Truth which finds
An echo in nigh all awakened minds.
And these illumined souls count in their rank
The enlightened of all lands who, from the plank
Of their own faith, leapt to the glorious height
From which diversity fades from one's sight
To manifest a state of oneness where
Consciousness reigns supreme both far and near.

How can you these avowals interpret,
Or any value on religion set
Save by admitting that the human soul
Is not a mere nonentity, a mole
Lost in the vast expanse of cosmic space,
A wisp of vapor one breath can efface,
A tiny flame extinguished by one gust
Of wind, a fragile mirror that break must?
But on the contrary the eternal base
Upon which stand the phantoms—time and space—
That weave the fabric of the huge expanse
Of all this world which, in the ecstatic trance,
Becomes a shadow, as compared to soul,
Now seen out-measuring it from pole to pole.

2
THE
LIMITATIONS OF INTELLECT

1

The priceless teaching of enlightened seers,
More so of ancient India, oft appears
Fantastic to skeptic intellects:
Some e'en ascribe it to the ill-effects
Of self-denial, carried to the extreme,
Excessive penance, lack of sleep and dream,
To solitude, diminished drink and food,
All working to cause a delusive mood.

Hence their alleged experience not a few
Ascribe to neuroses, of which they knew
Nothing, to fantasy, hypnotic trance,
To drugs, suggestion, mania, e'en to chance.
And thus rejected as false visionaries
Their influence on the crowd could not but cease.

But few of us imagine e'en in dream
That some among these seers have been the cream
Of earth, the guiding stars and beacon lights,
The first to soar to transcendental heights,
And gathering rare, intuitive knowledge there
Instructed mankind how to step with care
Upon the winding pathway, full of snares,
And pitfalls which can catch one unawares
To break a bone or but to feel a smart,
To take the lesson taught more to the heart.

The crisis facing all the race today
Is but a snare, encountered on the way,
To which conceited knowledge did not pay
Sufficient heed, because he turned too gay
And proud with his new skills in molding clay
And ore or having something new to say.
And so the actor who alone can play
This role in him, his soul, the immortal ray
Of life Divine, he pushed off far away.
The outcome: murdrous tempests brewing, nay
E'en cyclones threatening to destroy and slay.

The problem of pollution of the air,
Of earth and water which now causes a scare,
Among discerning intellects who see,
In it, a threat to all humanity,
All split up, in such an impossible way
And, at the moment, under such a sway
Of national rivalry, mistrust and hate,
That it should cause an outburst, soon or late.

To fight the evil on a global scale
Seems out of count—an effort that must fail.
For torn with hate, dissension, feud and spite,
Is there a grain of chance all would unite
To fight combinedly with mistrustless hearts
This all-corrupting hell before it starts?
The other threat: the ceaseless, wanton waste
Of earth's resources, done in foolish haste,

Is no less serious, for the lot of man
In future, for the still enormous span
Of time he is decreed to thrive on earth,
Cannot be happy if there is a dearth
Of ores and fossil products he now spends
Extravagantly e'en for frivolous ends.

Hence e'en if nature does not take in hand
Reform of what is now a robber band,
Depletion of essential ores will breed
Discord in those who have less than they need,
Adding another factor to invite
Hostility, contention, bloody fight,
All heading soon towards a global war,
Which to the visionless yet seems too far.

The recent short supply from oil-rich states
Has shown the world how such reduction grates,
The false assurances that science can find
Replacements for the products no more mined,
Trumpetted so loudly by some scholar teams,
Are vain, impracticable, deceptive dreams.
But can it help to impeach them one by one
When time is lost and all the damage done?

The gaudy raiment which now mankind wears
Does not conceal the poverty she bears,
The mind-distracting, soul-oppressing want
Of higher knowledge which alone can grant
That harmony and peace the world now lacks
And soon may make it stop dead in its tracks.

Alas, the erudite have no more clue
To what the present world-unrest is due
Than masses, and so flounder in the dark
Like others and, like them too, fail to mark
That grave disasters, threatening all the race,
Are omens she is now denied the Grace;
That Guardian Forces that protect her path
Towards her destination are in wrath.

47

Can e'en now knowledge make a timely guess
What makes its front-rank hasten to the Press,
And with loud cries and warnings cause alarm
Against pollution and the nuclear arm,
When it itself has given birth to both,
And proudly, after birth, sped up their growth?

All this in vain, the rot has spread so far
That naught, save Grace Divine or global war,
Can hold in check the galloping disease,
And wash out poisons the sick race to ease.

The danger which is now before their ken
Ought to have been anticipated when
They with stentorian voices loud proclaimed:
God is a myth and they have nature tamed;
When they made reason their unfailing guide
And final judge to settle and decide.

What is the end now of this loud acclaim?
Has nature been subdued or, oft with shame,
Some wise successors of the older team,
Who sense the threat and, like a shattered dream,
See all their world about to fall apart,
Because of gross mistakes done from the start?
In but a short span of a hundred years
Wrong proved the bombast that had first won cheers.

Because of this grave fault in intellect,
Which after centuries shows its effect,
Nature has planted another sense in man
The still hid distant future to scan.
But this prophetic eye can only adorn
Those who to a new dimension are reborn,
And through them Sovereign Life, in acts of Grace,
By means of Revelation guides the race;
A rare phenomenon in every age,
Which to the fore-front brought an illumined sage.

But still with these debacles well in sight,
Pollution on one side and nuclear fright

On another, birth-explosion on the third,
How many savants yet admit by word
Or deed that human intellect alone,
Howe'er in knowledge rich, at times, is prone
To grievous error, fatal at this stage
When, with man's climb into the nuclear age,
Explosive problems which ne'er met before
Can, with their urgency, now press him sore?

Among our Suns of knowledge is there one
Who knows that, with a little probing done,
It would be shortly proved beyond dispute
That there already is a charted route
Aligned for mankind, which it follow must
For all its span of life upon the crust
Of earth, and that to guide it on this Path
Comes Revelation to save it from scath?

But e'en those savants who, now wide awake
To these mistakes, ask one and all to take
Effective measures, in time, do not seem
To have themselves awakened from the dream,
Dear to the erudite, which makes them rate
Too highly their own scholarly estate;
And fallen victims to deceptive pride
What still they cannot judge in haste decide.

Oceans of learning nor a million books,
Nor all the teeming scholars of the earth,
Nor all technologists, whose future looks
So bright with their achievements of high worth,
Can e'er discover the mysterious cause
Of this distemper if, without a pause,
They toil and sweat for many years to unearth
The secret: which is spiritual dearth.

2

The search for our divine, immortal part,
Beyond the province of pure science, art

And e'en philosophy or other lore,
Demands a higher sphere of science more
Exact, elaborate and complex than
That which deals with the mortal side of man.

This probing of the secrets of our mind,
With knowledge, wisdom and research combined,
Will need a lengthy span of time to gain
Sufficient knowledge of the ethereal plane
Of consciousness to guide a seeker right,
With confidence, towards the illumining Light,
As now we can with some assurance guide
One in his plans about the physical side.

This science too will have its scope and plan,
Adepts and specialists who only can,
With higher channels of perception, find
What course of action suits the evolving mind
To keep it on the natural path decreed
By Heaven, with self-awareness as the meed.
To think a sudden revolution can
Bring Cosmic Consciousness to every man
Is to belie the record of the past
Which shows man ne'er could climb the ascent too fast.

Just as an infant grows to attain the stage
Of childhood, youth, maturity or age,
So has the race to accept her destiny,
Which modern intellect still fails to see,
And make herself familiar with the goal,
With its already writ, unchangeable scroll
Of Fate, of which no knowledge can be won
By intellect, whate'er the effort done.
For yet another sense transcending it
Has to be built up slowly, bit by bit,
By man with his own effort, to accord
With natural processes until the Lord
Of Life, enshrined within, wakes from his dream,
And soon transformed into a glorious beam

Of Life's Eternal Sun, wins to his goal
Of conscious oneness with the Unbounded Whole.

Born of our ignorance of cosmic laws,
Lack of this knowledge has caused and shall cause
Ills and distempers to the end of time,
Dissension, war, revolt, aggression, crime,
Which in the existing order ne'er can cease
And, as we see, with time must show increase
Until the earth looks like a seething sea
Of crime and blood-shed it has started to be.

These ills, like bodily ailments, have a cure
Which heaven already has provided for sure.
Unless obeyed now in the affairs of man
To cool down fires, which their defiance can fan,
Their further violation can but mean
A conflagration earth has never seen.
But nature keeps some secrets in her hold
Which only Revelation can unfold.

One learns them not in college nor in school,
Nor from the self-important men who rule
Nations, nor from the charlatans whose claims
Are born of selfish, merchandizing aims,
Nor from books that command colossal sales,
And make their flattered authors swell, like whales
With pride, while curious throngs race after them
To see their face, touch their hand, kiss their hem,
And charmers keep up a search with their eyes,
Eager to find if they can net the prize,
Or envious authors their earned millions count
And try to jog their own creative fount.

In vain, for save a Seer no mortal can
Unseal the laws that touch the Soul of man,
As here we come upon a province kept
Reserved by nature for the true adept,
Where nor the most accomplished scholar nor
The most exalted head can enter, for

This holy precinct is beyond the probe
Of those enamoured of the gown or robe.

The still extant Revealed directions came
Through mostly those who sought nor power nor fame,
And in the annals of mankind we see
That no one save a religious prodigy
Was e'er vouchsafed the rare, unequalled grace
Of chaste scriptural knowledge for the race.

What scholars, proud of their achievements, fail
To grasp is that a plane beyond the pale
Of intellect can ne'er become a theme
About which they can write or frame a scheme
Of study. This is why we often find
The chosen vehicle: an artless mind
Without that ponderous weight of learning which,
Instead of helping, proves a serious hitch.
Because a brain already over-taxed
By study cannot reach that calm, relaxed
And pure devotional frame in which alone
One can enraptured hear the inaudible tone
Of Cosmic Sound by which the awakened hears
The Wisdom, called Shruti by Vedic seers.

Awed by the august halo which surrounds
The Revelatory state, the ideas and sounds,
And the undreamed of change in consciousness,
It is no wonder those who won access
To this illumining, lofty state of Grace
Supposed that they with God were face to face.

Why Revelation often took the form
Of simple narrative, with its own charm,
Without embellishment and sophistry,
Of grandiosity and rhetoric free,
Is just because man in his heart of hearts
Loves pure simplicity, unspoiled by arts;
The target of his evolutionary drive,
His only way of life that can survive,

And he will have to purge himself with pain
Whene'er the lure of grandeur stunts his brain.

And hence to win to both man's head and heart
Simplicity supplies the highest art
For mass-appeal in palaces or slums,
The purpose for which Revelation comes,
Against the current false beliefs to shed
Illumining light to show the Path ahead,
Its turns and pitfalls, both in verse and prose,
Without pretension, in a measured dose,
With deep appeal to heart and reason free
To choose with what to differ or agree.

The testaments and scriptures of mankind,
Which have withstood the erosive stream of time
For centuries, both in the east and west,
For their appeal, effect and long-life rest
Not on adornment, sophistry or art,
But on their Message, dear to human heart.

Though written in a simple, artless style,
With no sophistication to defile,
And no maneuvering done for effect
To twist the teachings with which they are deckt,
They still command more credence and esteem
Than most books of our day whose authors seem
To revel in the thought that their own form
Of diction lacks no wise in grace and charm.

Full many a book with its perverted taste
In language, style or matter has laid waste
The idyllic beauty of the human mind
With false sophistication which we find
So rampant now, both in the high and low,
That one's true feeling it is hard to know.

Like huge industrial complexes which gloom
Pastoral loveliness, the honest bloom,
Native to man's mind, which depends in main,
On right behaviour of the evolving brain,

Is being steadily eroded by
Our own mistaken efforts when we try
To orientate our writing with the aim
To win applause, admirers, wealth or fame.

But few accomplished writers of our time,
Acknowledged master-hands at prose or rhyme,
Display awareness of the simple fact
That printed words on mortal mind react
With such force and intensity they can
Ennoble or debase it quicker than
E'en good or evil company can do
To millions of confiding readers who,
Enamoured of the style, are borne away
Towards erroneous thinking every day.

Whene'er true Revelation came it chose
Its own semantic channel which made those,
Lost in the wilds of intellectual doubt,
Proud of their worth, to run it down and shout,
Denouncing its alleged defects and faults.
But since Truth waxes stronger with assaults
Their loud outcry too helped serve nature's aim
To spread the Message and confirm its claim,
While their dissenting notes were swept aside
By Time, as straw is by a rushing tide.

When reason is bombarded heavily
With specious logic and fallacious plea
In ceaseless volleys of pedantic words,
Of words and words, it soon is torn to shreds,
And with a heavy dose of scholarship,
If not on guard, is often prone to slip
Into what the author likes it to believe,
With little choice to examine it and sieve,
Till a fresh barrage from another book
To the first impress gives an altered look.

Temporal knowledge, wareless of the goal
Decreed by nature for man and his soul;

The glorious summit he shall reach at last,
As every faith has in some way forecast,
Howe'er colossal, rich, amazing, sure,
Which of immoderate lust can find no cure,
Can be as dangerous as neglected fire
That warms but can destroy the hearth entire.

This is what Maitri Upanishad says about true knowledge:[1]
"Who is the bird of golden hue,
Who dwells in both the heart and sun,
Swan, diver-bird, surpassing bright—
Him let us worship in this fire! . . .

As fire, of fuel destitute
Becomes extinct in its own source,
So thought by loss of activeness
Becomes extinct in its own source.

Becomes extinct in its own source,
Because the mind the Real seeks!
For one confused by things of sense,
There follow action's false controls.

Samsara is just one's own thought;
With effort he should cleanse it, then.
What is one's thought, that he becomes;
This is the eternal mystery.

For by tranquility of thought,
Deeds, good and evil, one destroys.
With soul serene, stayed on the Soul,
Delight eternal one enjoys . . .

So long the mind should be confined,
Till in the heart it meets its end.
That is both knowledge and release!
All else is but a string of words!

---

[1]Maitri Upanishad 6.34 and 7-8, translated by R.E. Hume

With mind's stains washed away by concentration,
What may his joy be who has entered Atman—
Impossible to picture then in language!
Oneself must grasp it with the inner organ . . . .

By the jugglery of a doctrine that denies the soul,
By false comparisons and proofs
Disturbed, the world does not discern
What is the difference between knowledge and ignorance"

This from the third Patriarch of Zen:[1]
"Wordiness and intellection—
The more with them, the further astray we go;
Away therefore with wordiness and intellection,
And there is no place where we cannot pass freely.

When we return to the root, we gain the meaning;
When we pursue external objects we lose the reason.
The moment we are lightened within,
We go beyond the voidness of a world confronting us."

This from Rumi:
"Before the city of perfect wisdom these senses are like
the donkeys of the oilpress, whose eyes are blind-folded."
Again:
"So long as man comes not out of his senses,
he remains ignorant of transcendent entities."

Words and words in a thousand bulky books
A day, all o'er the earth, like baited hooks
Attract and scatter with consummate art
People, in this age of the nuclear dart,
Into assemblies of mistrustful hearts,
And hundreds of antagonistic parts.

Most books on national issues, sects and creeds,
Now as abundant as exuberant weeds

[1]Manual of Zen-Buddhism by D.T. Suzuki

56

Are in a garden, left untrimmed to grow
As lush as they can, like fast-gathering snow,
More often try to separate and divide,
To extol demerits e'en and add to pride,
Instead of making wide appeals to unite
To save life, wealth and culture from the blight
Of bias, hate, discordance, lastly war
Which spells death of all we are striving for.

3

It might be argued that religious zeal
Has caused more injury than it could heal,
Inflicted suffering, ignorance and want,
And done its utmost in our mind to plant
Dark superstition and irrational myth,
So crass it has to be contended with
E'en now, and prejudice so deep ingrained
That e'en the learned, who have insight gained
Into the equal worth of every faith,
Their own religion still superior rate,
With the result that mankind e'en now stands
Divided on religion in all lands.

Again the idea that consciousness alone
Is the reality and what is known
As matter has no firm, substantial base,
Attended by or devoid of time and space,
Does not fit in with the observed facts
For there is something which acts and reacts
On mind, external to it that creates
The complex world we see in wakeful states,
Complete with mass and movement, time and space,
Of which we all the components can trace.

When we observe the puny human mind
In cretins, in the insane, the deaf and blind,
We see how foolish, blind and queer, at times,
It can be, or how prone to sin and crimes.

And then with remedies applied with skill
The blind can see and deaf with music thrill.
These undeniable facts so clearly seen
None can regard as an illusive scene.

The world around built with the progress made
Lately is not a phantom nor a shade;
But hard reality which only came
To be when honest savants lit the flame
Of reason and with it soon chased away
The shades of superstition holding sway,
Both o'er the faithful masses and their priests,
Who often made the former bend, like beasts
Of burden, to all that their faith decreed,
And blindly rope to it their thought and deed,
With threats of dire award from heaven if they,
Ensnared by flesh, were e'er to go astray.

All o'er the earth the powerful priestly clan
Erected uncanny worlds of myth in man
Of heavens and hells, of angels, devils and
Other fictitious tribes in many a land,
Until all feared and most of them yet fear
The wrath of heaven puissant everywhere.

They bade experiment and research to keep
Within the bounds of faith's permissible sweep,
And make the truths uncovered stay within
Her holy precincts to keep safe their skin.

They forced submissive knowledge not to move
Beyond the edges of the hallowed groove,
And thus confined within the narrow bounds
Of one book or a few with closed compounds
The sure result could not be but to stunt
The growth of mind, to deaden it and blunt!

The light of reason which, not shed before
In fullness, kept man famished, sick and sore,
In worlds of suffering, darkness, want and fear,
Of hard, exhausting toil with primitive gear,

Oppressive rulers, heartless lieges and lords,
Travel so risky that one needed guards,
Movement so tardy one in months could make
A journey which now but some hours can take,
Diseases rampant, ignorance so wide
All lived in awe of elements, wind and tide.
In short, a gloomy world bereft of all
Modern amenities we oft recall
With pride, as products of a fruitful age
When reason, not religion, holds the stage.

The blooming, opulent world before our eyes
Never attained to this exuberant size
To this abundance of luxurious goods,
Of fancy garments and delicious foods,
Of every comfort and convenience which
Nor e'en great kings could dream of, nor the rich,
All done when science and reason both dictate
The course of human destiny and fate,
Free from the tentacles of mythical thought,
Dogmatic trash and superstitious rot!

It would be idle to dispute the stand
That since the time, when reason took command
Of various spheres of knowledge, there has been
A marvellous change in the earthly scene.
What were diseased and famine-stricken lands,
Icy tracts, marshy wastes and desert sands,
Converted into idyllic heavens in bloom,
Into bright sunshine, have emerged from gloom.

But all these victories you proudly claim
Arose from nowhere save the intelligent Flame
Of Consciousness, the one primordial base
Of all gifts that adorn the human race.

Nor search nor scholarship nor earth nor stone
Nor metal but all-knowing Life alone
Has been the one unfailing constant source
Of all these triumphs, with all its **Pranic** force,

Of all our progress, all those fertile lands,
Reclaimed from frozen wastes and barren sands,
Those factories and large industrial plants,
Tall skyscrapers, which make men look like ants,
Those luxury ships, streamlined railway trains,
Attractive cars and mammoth aeroplanes;
Computers, television, movies and
All other marvels, always close at hand.

Imposing bridges, delightful glossy roads,
House-hold appliances in huge cartloads,
Engineering triumphs, architectural feats,
Freedom of action which all record beats,
Unequalled medical and surgical skill
In curing sickness, otherwise sure to kill,
Adding to health and strength, prolonging life
With nigh infallible remedies now rife,
In short, a most delightfully altered earth
For man to live in plenty, joy and mirth;
A new world with new hope, ambition, thought,
An earthly paradise which reason wrought.

It is creative Life whose breast supplied
The milk of reason which became the guide
Of mankind in a long, historic march
To lead, at last, to our triumphal-arch.

How rationalists demolished faith in God
And o'er religious concepts rode rough-shod,
Is clear from Thomas Huxley's curt remark
Which shows how reason can err, e'er in dark
About what future will prove true or fake
And what turn human life and thought would take,
When he condemned the natural urge in man
To fashion God in his own image than
Upon an inconceivable model, not
Accessible readily to human thought.

He ne'er could visualize the change ahead
When sure of his own still wet ground he said[1]
That men forgive all injuries save those
Which touch their self esteem, and so they chose
To make their gods in their own likeness and
In their own image (equal with them to stand).

Influenced by the currents of our day,
We think the same ideas would e'er hold sway,
Forgetting oft the lesson of the past
That change is rooted in our mental cast,
And nature uses it to work out her plan,
Taking advantage of this trait in man.
Revival of a growing interest in
Religion and the world of life within
Denotes a change in trends that had begun
In Huxley's time and have their tenure run,
And clearly shows how purblind we can be
When dealing with the eternal mystery.

What Huxley failed to see, in self-conceit
Sure of his ground, is that the attempt to treat
Man as a chance-met foundling in a world
So inconceivably vast that he is hurled
Into the low position of a worm
Can only damp his spirit and confirm
The hold of weak, defeatist trends in him
Which mock at things sublime and treat as whim
With no ideals faith alone can gift
His soul to acknowledge, honour and uplift:
Ideals which despite the hammer-blows
Of reason, still in human breast repose,
Instilled by faith, for save the idea of soul
And God, naught else man's strong lust can control.

Where then the love of justice, goodness, truth,
Of charity, benevolence and ruth?

---

[1]The Evolution of Theology, by T.H. Huxley.

Where then the dream of making life sublime
Or patriotic thought for one's own clime?
Where then the impulse not to be so small
As to deceive one or from virtue fall?
Where then the care of neighbour and mankind
Only which hearts in harmony can bind?
Where then the golden rules of conduct which
Restrain from yielding blindly to the itch
Of wrong desire, brute force or moral vice,
Which oft exact a most disastrous price
As they have started now to do apace
To warn mankind she is debarred from grace
For violation of the Eternal Law,
From which alone she can protection draw.

What else can we expect when we reduce
Man to the level of a carnal brute,
Din into him that he is born of dust
With no eternal bond he honour must,
Between him and the cosmos as a whole,
Provided by his own immortal soul?

To isolate him from his cosmic base
Is to deny him his exalted place
He holds by right, though chained by space and time,
As true heir to a legacy sublime,
An heirdom he should ne'er let out of view
And always meditating on it live,
Till his own being is pervaded by
The thought of his Divinity, to try
In his behaviour, mode of thought and act
To live the life till it becomes a fact.

They but deceived themselves and all the world
And mankind into a grave dilemma hurled,
Suspicious of religion, who denied
Divinity to soul and wrongly tried
To give to Mammon precedence over God,
To down-grade and identify with sod
What in their arrogance they failed to scan,
The sovereign province of the soul of man.

Allured by senses they assigned to them
The state supreme of Life's immortal gem—
The soul to them so weak and fragile seemed
That they it of but little import deemed,
And on the false assumption that at death
It is extinguished with the parting breath,
Applied their thought and skill to pamper flesh,
To keep the body always young and fresh,
And in this vain endeavour steered the race
Towards a maelstrom which now nears apace.

4

O scholars of the earth pray do awake
From your Utopias ere upheavals shake
The world, reducing all your store to ash
With wrathful Life's one all-destroying flash.
For lost in matter's vast deceptive show,
You fail to realize what you should know,
That this one spark of consciousness in you,
Which often spurs you on to find out "Who
You are," is a live ember from a Fire
That holds in but one coign the world entire—
This giant cosmos of earths, moons and stars,
Whose image you, from your own study, bars.

Should not your wisdom hallowed by the fire
Of long experience tell you and inspire
To ponder deeply, with a sober head,
What is the source of all that you have read,
What you know, fancy, reason out or think?
That keeps alert and active when you sink
In sleep, takes care of larynx when you talk,
And hundreds of your muscles when you walk
Or run, digests your food, allots due share
To organs, flesh and blood with scrupulous care?
And when oblivious to the world you sleep,
Repairs and tones the brain to make that sweep

63

Of thought which spans far off stars, deepest sea
And highest knowledge, both in you and me,
Imbued with fires which may, for all we know,
In future on some distant planet glow.

Much of our knowledge is but sorry fare,
Served in elaborate trays that cause a scare
Among the half-read, who with awe peruse
Books which of words and names make lavish use.
Hence e'en a serious study of such books
Most of the readers leaves with vacant looks,
Still baffled by the riddle of their life,
Still conscious e'en when deeply sunk in strife
That hundreds of works read have not allayed
Their thirst nor e'en rewarded the effort made
To find out whether their mysterious "I"
Is of immortal stuff or born to die.

The reason why the mystery of life
Is still unsolved, despite the theories rife,
Despite research and study by the learned
Of global fame, despite the laurels earned,
Is that e'en authors of world-wide repute
On the phenomena of life are mute,
Or, at the best, express conflicting views
Which valued one day soon are vapid news,
After a brief sensation dying down
Into the oblivious sea of time to drown.

The fault lies in the wishful thinking. dear
To those academic distinctions wear
For whom the still-augmenting ponderous weight
Of current knowledge oft acts as a bait
To lure them readily to the false belief
That for awareness of self too the chief
Lever is knowledge and more knowledge still
To reach the goal and, if not, then to kill
The very spirit of enquiry in
The mind when it is made a book-worm bin.

If books and learning were to grant relief
To souls' consuming thirst and bring belief
To those assailed by spiritual doubt,
Or show from their dilemmas the way out,
Then all the standing load of books on earth,
Enough to weave a broad belt round her girth,
Or, if piled up together in a heap,
Enough to make a mountain, high and steep,
Should have sufficed full many times o'er
To bring to light what still lies under co'er.

Then why should ardent souls search far and wide
If books could keep them the least satisfied,
And why, renouncing family, comfort, home
Myriads of seekers all the earth should roam
To assuage this scorching thirst that grants no rest
To those who have it burning in their breast?

Why then should many a scholar widely read,
With high distinction, whose fame far has spread,
When brooding on himself, with tearful eyes
And folded hands, look wistfully at the skies,
Seeking for an answer to the riddle most
Near to his heart, in life's enigma lost.

Since Socrates and Vasishta had their say
Which solace grants to millions e'en today,
Since Upanishads, the Bible and Quran
All pointed out the way to a glorious dawn,
To a new awareness in the human soul,
About its Maker and its Sovereign Goal,
Why has not one known scholar, with the same
Assurance, with all his success and name,
Been able to convince the searching crowd
That he too is with Light Divine endowed?

Again, of all these giants of the past,
Who, like the pole star still their luster cast,
How many, ere they lit the illumining flame,
Had earned for learning a distinguished name?

Of e'en the stars of lesser magnitude,
The sages, seers and mystics all imbued
With the same spirit, though in brilliance less,
Hundreds in count, how many did possess
That wealth of secular knowledge which adorns
A modern intellectual who oft mourns
His lack of calm and peace, e'en falling prey
To paranoiac trends so rife today.

What solace does it bring if after years
Of onerous study till the body wears,
In loading the mind with fact after fact
Until so full it does not ev'n react,
And later loads in order to have room
Consign the former to oblivious gloom,
The aging pedant now with senile brain,
Despite his load of books, recalls with pain
That he knows no more of life, save in name,
At his departure time than when he came.

Do we not see that those who read too much
Become accustomed, like the lame to a crutch,
In their discourses to support their talk,
As a leaf is supported by its stalk,
With phrases and quotations from the books
They have devoured and still with avid looks
Search for some more to fill the hungry brain,
Which ne'er without a new book can remain
At rest, displaying a sorry state of mind,
In its own mansion which no peace can find.

If books and depth of learning—viewed apart
From their utility in science, art
And other spheres of knowledge—could provide
For leading to Divine, a trusty guide
It would prove that it is the natural course
For hungry souls to reach the Eternal Source
Of their existence, and those who excel
In knowledge and not others would then swell

The number of the Enlightened and attain
To self-awareness with temporal gain.

But far from it we see the opposite,
And it is seldom that a learned wit
Or prodigy in knowledge won access
To occult domains of nature or could press
The Powers that be to open wide the door,
Through which he could proceed a little more,
Beyond the boundaries of corporeal thought,
To reach the rare transcendent regions sought.

Much though our knowledge is now on the increase,
And gifted authors, like untiring bees,
In torrents new ideas and doctrines pour
To turn the earth into a honey-store,
Yet it is obvious that the boon we need
More than the exciting books, we daily read
Is of serene reflection's calming dose
To keep our fretful minds more in repose.

Can any scholar now a forecast make
At what point of our progress we would wake
To self-awareness, mental poise and calm,
To prove the worth of learning as a balm,
For mankind and not, as we see today,
Its prowess only to drive both away,
Leaving unrest the hero of the day.

If no one can predict this, does it mean
That, after studying well the human scene,
The bloody wars and carnage of our time,
Increase in violence, aggression, crime,
Knowledge still cannot show a safe way out
Of this alarming state it knows about.

In actual fact, does it not also mean
That save as mere spectator of the scene,
Of human effort, suffering, hope and fear,
Knowledge possesses no power, distinct and clear,

67

Save with the learned batteries it erects,
To bring peace to the soul, remove defects
And, with research and study done, to guide
The eager crowds to self-awareness wide.

Indeed, if knowledge has power, as is said,
Then how can it be that when so wide-spread,
And so oceanic, the earth has become
A live volcano, clearly seen by some
Among the foremost of the learned ranks,
Distinguished scholars, not alarmist cranks,
Who let no chance escape to make this known:
The world explosive and unsafe has grown.

It might be argued that as things now stand
The erudite have not the slightest hand
In shaping the lives and affairs of men,
Save by advice with spoken word or pen,
Which guides the rulers as well as the ruled
Through study, precept or when trained and schooled.

But are the erudite themselves aware
Of what demands their foremost thought and care:
Whither the human caravan is bound?
To reach some goal or on an aimless round?
Is there some purpose which it must fulfill,
To which it should subserve its thought and will?
Or is it free to do whate'er it likes
Whate'er it thinks out or its fancy strikes?
Is it a fragment of an aimless whole
Or meant to act a pre-allotted role?

This is a vital issue they needs must
Decide before hand to command the trust
Of people in what they do or design
With their inherent trends to be in line:
The pivot on which every scheme and plan
Which they frame for the betterment of man
Must hinge, if they wish to keep knowledge free
From the ignoble stain of quackery.

Because what they prescribe for human weal,
Our wants to satisfy, our ills to heal,
Can ne'er be to the mark unless they can
Correctly diagnose the state of man;
Unless they know the natural trends innate
In human bodies and their course locate,
Unless they first decide with thought and skill
Is mankind static or evolving still?
And, if the latter, for what distant aim
Has nature fashioned her organic frame?

Without an answer to the questions posed,
Whate'er is planned at present or proposed
For future, done in utter ignorance
Of natural targets set for man's advance,
Cannot be reckoned more dependable than
The dubious nostrums of a charlatan.

Or, at the best, unskilled attempts to find
By trial and error methods, like the blind,
What things do not agree and what things suit
The crowd on the unfamiliar, tortuous route:
Haphazard methods which one moment right
The next can be as deadly as a blight
And land the race in awful crises, sure
To cause distress with little hope of cure,
As is about to happen to remind
The elite they still to nature's ways are blind.

5

Knowledge has come to mean, among the learned
Of our day, grades, degrees, diplomas earned,
As means to wealth, position, power and fame
Which not unoft fetch it a tarnished name;
Or seas of learning with minute detail
Of any branch of study, head to tail;

Or worlds of information more and more
Extended with additions to the store,
Till it grows to encyclopaedian size,
So that all there is on earth or the skies
Is always bursting from one's finger tips,
Ready for prompt expression on his lips;
Confined to what we round us hear and see
With not a word to our own mystery!

And e'en the towering giants of this class
Show not the slightest merit to surpass
The unlettered masses in what is most near,
Most precious, most essential and most dear
To man, the wisdom leading to his soul;
His one immortal asset whole and sole.

How then can Knowledge e'er achieve the aim
For which we honour it, for which we came,
To lead a happy life and leave again
Enlightened that we did not come in vain,
And are not parting with as empty hands
As we came with, like water lost in sands?
That on an earth of such colossal size
We did not pass our time, like butterflies,
Like them, despite the skill to roam the skies,
Lived not unmindful, till we closed our eyes,
Of our true destiny and our main aim,
What is this all about and why we came?

If man and his achievements since he came
Are doomed to perish, like a blown-out flame,
Reducing life's drama to a farce,
A gloomy ending for e'en leading stars,
It means we acquit ourselves no better than
The clumsy, now-extinct reptilian clan
Of Dinosaurs, which vanished clean away
After some million years of wasted stay,
And with all our great deeds at last shall die,
As void of knowledge as the void of sky,

70

About the purpose of our own debut
Upon this stage, about our goal and route.

Can e'en the touch of Midas compensate
For loss of sight, if so decreed by Fate?
Or can unbounded knowledge, skill and wealth
Repay the loss of sanity and health?
Or can exciting trips to Mars or Moon
Or full possession of earth's every boon
Remove the uncertainty and fear of death
Which shadows human life to the last breath?
If not, then Knowledge will but pave the way
To low, hedonist modes of life which may
Corrupt the thinking soon of all mankind
If we no answer to the Riddle find.

How can temporal knowledge be of help
And make up for our blindness to our Self?
How can its great discoveries and exploits
Bestow serenity and quell the riots
Inside our mind and feelings when we brood
Upon ourselves in a reflective mood?
Returning with a sigh to daily chores
To doubt-tormented lives ourselves to force!

Who can deny the unmatched, impressive role
Which knowledge has played and can play to mould
Man's life and thought, environment and earth
With contributions of the highest worth?
Who can deny the truth that only it
Can fertilize our intellect and wit,
Open horizons of progressive thought
And guide to new ideals to be brought
Within the compass of accomplished dreams,
Equip for better and still better schemes,
In short, with right direction of the mind
Towards a richer life can all incline?

But it no power has o'er desire and lust,
Nor o'er ambition nor the stormy gust

Of passion nor e'en o'er the urge to rule,
To Lord o'er and exploit the weak and fool.
Nor on the rulers has it any hold,
Nor on the ruled, towards their conscience cold,
When they within the letter of the law,
Commit such crimes that it is hard to draw
A picture of the outrageous acts of shame
Done both by commons and those with a name,
Though well-informed, well-read and well-behaved,
Yet in the depths of mind by vice enslaved.

What can be done with such invincible foes
Of law and order who extremely close
Are e'er on fire to launch such strong attacks
That e'en a strong wall of resistence cracks?

What profit can accrue in the long run
If riotous lust, e'er ready with a gun,
Demolishes all that knowledge has achieved,
To leave eroded mankind sorely grieved?

What profit can accrue if all the race,
In progress keen to accelerate her pace,
The masses toiling to make two ends meet,
With ceaseless effort to stand on their feet
Morning and evening, when free from their task,
Glad in the warmth of their hearth to bask,
One happy in his child, other in his mate,
Content with simple fare, resigned to Fate,
Mistrustless that some one's demoniac lust
For power or wealth their heaven can bring to dust,
And one day frozen with fright make them see
What ghastly end of their life had to be.

What profit can accrue if, after all
That knowledge has done to remove the pall
Of ignorance that once enslaved the race,
And kept in bonds want and distress to face
It, with the left hand hastens to destroy
What with the right it lends to fill with joy;

When, like a sharp two-edged sword it can smite,
To suit its choice both to the left and right,
Placing a weapon in unscrupulous hands
That can reduce the earth to a sea of sands?

If knowledge cannot mould the lust of man,
But lavishly supplies him all it can,
How long can we expect him to resist
The urge to rob, to grab or use his fist
As he is doing now and e'er has done?
Degraded multitudes to exalt but one,
Despoiled a populace to enrich a few,
Decried old wisdom to say something new,
Designed a massacre to let one live,
Discredited millions to defend one view,
Dealt death to legions one a crown to give,
Denied to myriads peace a war to brew
To appease his lust to kill, to hack and hew.
In short, whene'er it did his purpose suit,
With wit he justified acts of a brute.

Replete with knowledge, lust, adept in craft,
Such logic can employ, such sermons draft
That, what to say of crowds, whole nations can
Become unconscious dupes of but one man;
A hazardous experiment in this age,
When earth-destroying weapons are the rage,
When lines of experts sit, absorbed in thought,
How to devise the ideal weapon sought
Unerringly which, ere reprisals, can
Wipe off a hostile land to the last man,
Relying on knowledge and more knowledge still
To cause a fresh sensation, one more thrill,
When media loud announce the invention made,
An affront to God, of madness the first shade!

Can academic knowledge know or check,
Unnoticed, if the whole race runs amuck,
Duped by the specious logic of a few,
With itch for power or other aim in view,

And fights a world war for their gain or fame,
Tricked by the genius of a tarnished flame
Of consciousness, no medicine can cure
And no precaution remedy ensure.

Those who believe in Truth, with faith in God,
If they are honest and do not defraud
Their cherished principles or conscience kill,
How can they lend assent or bend their will
To advance the growth of nuclear arsenals,
A blacker crime than that of cannibals;
To atrocious measures, what-so-e'er the need
Which make a mockery of faith and creed,
Tear off the mask of pretense from the face
Not only of a part but all the race,
Show it in its true colour as a lost
And doomed creation which, to pay the cost
Of its ill-pampered lust, contrived its doom,
Just when it had attained a glorious bloom,
To satisfy the mania of a few
Whose **Pranic** Spectrum somehow is askew.

Howe'er advanced, how knowledge can avert
The over-hanging menace and assert
Its dominance, when it too is a prey
To same disorders, it should keep away,
When its own arrogant, dogmatic trains
Show of the same affection patent strains,
And holding to a certain point of view,
A theory or a doctrine, old or new,
To safeguard their conviction or their aim,
Or e'en the source of profit or their fame
Oppose another concept, tooth and nail,
If it disputes theirs or prevents its sale.

Could any scholar fifty years before
Foresee the problems which now press us sore:
The problems of unrest among the young,
Who more intelligent and more highly strung,

74

Demand a better social order for
The whole of mankind with no threat of war?

The problem of division in the ranks
Of strife-torn mankind: Some for guns and tanks
And some for amity, but all combined,
Proving a danger for our peace of mind;
Also a danger to the safety of
The race, for who knows when the sky may drop
Atomic showers to drown in streams of blood
The whole of mankind ravaged by the flood?

The problem of explosion in the rate
Of population growth which, soon or late,
If not controlled in time, may well assume
A grave proportion when with limited room
The overcrowded earth becomes a place
Of frightful carnage for mere standing space,
For mere one or two frugal meals a day
To keep sure death from hunger just away.

The problem of pollution is as grave
As war and pestilence; for what can save
The health and sanity of mankind when
The earth become a filthy, reeking fen
With lethal water and envenomed fumes
Of air, her strength and energy consumes?
Until the daily poisoned race succumbs
To the infection which e'en now benumbs
The teeming crowds of large industrial towns,
And in a sea of toxic vapour drowns.

And no less serious is the loss of ores
And metals whose extraction we now force
Most injudiciously, lost to all sense
Of prudence, only to hoard pounds and pence,
Heedless that nature has kept this reserve
For ages mankind's moderate need to serve,
And not to be consumed in senseless ways,
Like rapidly dissolved fire-work displays.

Before the elite there still is looming large
The post-Renaissance, ill-conceived mirage
Which lured those pioneers towards a trap
Of progress, that still holds us in its lap,
A vain mirage, evoked by carnal lust,
To wallow like an animal in the dust
Of pleasures which delight, excite and thrill,
Enervate body and the spirit kill.

This makes us squander our material wealth,
As culpably as if despoiled by stealth,
To keep in humour, plenty, comfort, trim,
A still immature race and put this whim
Into her head that she is free to rule
And do whate'er she likes to exhaust or pool
The treasures nestling in earth's mining tracts,
As if omniscient Eyes watch not her acts.

Grossly misguided and betrayed, the race
Ev'n at this crucial hour displays no trace
Of caution, though approaching from all sides
Grave crises and disasters rush, like tides;
Visible to all: The rulers and the mobs,
The unread and scholars, the humble and the snobs;
All in suspense, torn between hope and fear.
How will it climax? Is war far or near?
And lost in these conjectures but few know
That nature's Instruments, ordained to mow
The human crop, like standing fields of corn,
Hitlers and Ghengis Khans have since been born!

Not for revenge, that ne'er can be the aim
Of the compassionate Lord, but to reclaim
A fallen angel, wandering from his path
To glory, drawing upon himself the wrath
Of nature, as a child provokes the ire
Of parents, when it wilfully plays with fire!

What else can you suggest to slow the pace
Of now the hopelessly besotted race,

76

Rushing towards a doom she cannot sight,
As her hilarious mood denies the light,
Towards degeneration and decay
Which every vanished culture swept away,
And would destroy our being too for sure,
If nature, well in time, applies no cure.

One single remedy for all the faults
By which mankind now her advancement halts:
One single blow to vanquish and kick out
The demon of agnosticism and doubt:
One single lesson to keep us alert
That earth's chaste cradle is not soiled with dirt:
One single warning to make us desist
From warfare, hatred and the rule of fist.

One single shaking to make us aware
That just as parents for their children spare
Whate'er they can to make their future smooth,
We too must keep in mind the future youth
And not deprive them, to indulge our lust,
Of assets which we for them hold in trust.

One single penalty to help us sight:
We are not safe unless we all unite
To meet the challenge of the nuclear age
And of our progress write a golden page,
When all agree to save the lives we waste
In war to keep alive a savage taste.

One rocking tremor of the earth can right
Our thinking, our internal darkness light,
Destroy illusions of conceit and pride
And show on what a fragile base we bide,
E'er at the mercy of the invincible might
Of nature, suffered whether wrong or right.

Likewise upheavals which convulse the frame
Of mankind, millions kill and millions maim,

Proceed from flouted Consciousness to force
Unheeding multitudes to change their course
Of life, and set their thought and conduct right,
When they grow dead to her resistless might,
And act in ways which tend to undermine
Her plan to make imperfect man divine,
Then either self-correction done apace
Can only save from suffering or her Grace.

3

WHAT IS
COSMIC CONSCIOUSNESS

1

When rid of fetters which soul freedom bar
I am borne swiftly, like a feather, far
And far away, towards the sun and moon,
With senses still alert and not in swoon,
With thought subdued, but more alive within,
Oblivious to surrounding noise and din
When not too loud, for I soon feel withdrawn
From my corporeal frame of flesh and brawn.
Then light as air and bright as sunshine roam,
From one end to the other, the ambient dome.

Where am I now, who earlier felt himself
Completely shut up in a narrow shelf,
With no awareness of his sorry plight,
Like that of an imprisoned ray of light,
Or beaming splendour tight shut in a box,
Or ravishing beauty hid behind an ox?

Where am I when I look down from aloft
And watch my living body, warm and soft?
Half bound to it by some invisible link
For while I float around I also think;
A conscious Titan of unmeasured size,
Still hearing with his ears, seeing with his eyes,
Aware yet of his presence everywhere,
A puny man, also a cosmic seer.

What marvel is this, what unique estate?
How did I merit this rare boon from fate?
Attired in vestments of empyrean light
My own ethereal person greets my sight,
From every object in the void of space
As if I hold creation in embrace.

Far from the thoughts of earth, beyond the pale
Of every sorrow mortals can assail,
A living ocean of discarnate life
Serene, beyond all stress, away from strife,
Not that embodied "I" of narrow girth,
But a colossus measuring heaven and earth;
A giant awareness stretching far and near
As highly conscious here as it is there.

A strange sensation I feel through and through
Reflected when I see myself in you,
And your whole person, figure, face and all
Looks like a picture in the open hall
Of my awareness which enshrining you,
Both inside and out, shows we are not two,
But one, formed of the same amazing stuff
That seen as matter seems so hard and rough.

In full alertness, nor asleep nor drunk,
I feel detached from body, head and trunk,
Only a vague sort of remembrance ties
Me to the flesh and senses, ears and eyes,
But for the rest spread out on every side
In every point of compass I reside,

A lustrous beam compounded with the scene
Which it surveys, the seer become the seen.

For reasons of which yet I am not sure,
But maybe when the nerves are rendered pure,
And **Prana** freely pours into the brain,
Breaking the spatial and temporal chain,
I find myself in heaven, more than a king,
So filled with ecstasy I dance and sing,
In all abandon, like a spouting fount
Whose waters spread out widely as they mount,
Linked to the body by a slender thread,
I fill the whole span of sky over-head.

What can possession, power and riches mean
To one who has with awe and wonder seen
Himself alive in disembodied form,
Immune to fire, untouched by rain and storm;
A bodiless mind, from cramping ego free,
Of vast expanse, as far as one can see,
Void of desire and lust, free from the sway
Of passion, spread both near and far away,
With thought as steady, intellect as keen,
Observing carefully the impossible scene:
A drop, expanding o'er the surface of
An ocean, while its waters wave and toss,
Become perceptive of the whole expanse,
At this astounding feat to laugh and dance.

Imagine that you press in close embrace
A sweetheart, your ideal of form and face,
Tasting most exquisite thrill after thrill
Of swooning rapture, as long as you will,
Conscious the whole time of her ravishing charm,
Voluptuous throbbing body, soft and warm,
Pressing hard, panting, as if dying to unite
With you in one prolonged throb of delight,
Oblivious to the world and all it holds
As every moment a new joy unfolds,
While time stands still in an unending now
And thought dissolves in one blaze of love,

Leaving alone before the ravished mind
Unbounded rapture with no thorn behind.

Now picture, with this transport in your mind,
A vast awareness which no limits bind,
Akin to an ocean of bliss stretching far,
With no restriction anywhere to bar
Your own expansion in this deep until,
Enfolding all you see, the plain and hill,
And all the immense stretch of the world in you,
Not as an outer but an inner view,
You swim in such a flood of joy, as if
The whole of nature, no more hard and stiff,
Become a melting lass hugs you to kiss,
Drenching herself and you with streams of bliss,
So that the Seer and the Seen unite
In one long-drawn thrill of supreme delight.

Can life a more intense enjoyment give,
Ready at hand, as long as one does live,
The acme of delight which ne'er will cloy,
And e'er with added thrill one can enjoy,
No sign of weakness, no exhaustion feel
While senses with the flood of transport reel.

Such have been oft the ecstatic thrills of those
Who as enlightened seers and prophets rose,
Drunk with intoxicating love divine
More heady than the most exciting wine,
Yet keeping mind alert and wit intact
To know that this Elysium is a fact.
What they experienced in the rapturous trance
Excels the transports of love and romance.

No wonder that the ravished senses swoon,
And midnight changes into brilliant noon,
All gloomy thoughts, like shadows of the night,
Dissolve at once in this entrancing light,
And leave the mind unoccupied with aught,
Suggesting e'en remotely painful thought.

"Supreme joy fills the yogi who has gained[1]
Freedom from sin" Says Gita "and attained
Union with Brahma, who his mind has weaned
From turbulent passion and its flow serened."

"He who is here in man's organic mould[2]
Is also in the sun" So we are told
In Taittiriya Upanishad; "and one
Who from his flesh and world release has won
Attains to bodies made of Prana, mind
And intellect, supreme Bliss last to find."

"From the beginning revelations take[3]
Such flagrant shapes that while yet wide awake"
Says Al-Ghazzali, "Sufis see before
Them angels and the souls of prophets, they
E'en hear their voices and for favours pray.
The Transport rises to such high degree
From all the forms and figures which they see,
That it defies expression and without
Incurring sin no one may leak it out."

"Throughout, in every stage of prayer, I[4]
Have mentioned though some work is put in by
The gardener;" Says Saint Teresa, "But in
The later stages one can feel within
Such Bliss and comfort with the labour done
That soul would ne'er abandon once 'tis won.
Labour is no more felt as labour then
But as Bliss so unutterable that when
Partaken of such rare joy fills the heart
That all the senses cease to do their part,
And save this one enjoyment soul does not
During the spell think any other thought,

_____

[1]Bhagwad Gita VI-27
[2]Taittiriya Upanishad II.8.5
[3]M. Schmolder's translation of Al-Ghazzalis autobiography.
[4]Life of Saint Teresa

And though enjoying it still is not wise
From where such all-consuming joy can rise."

"I, Lalla, entered by the garden-door[1]
Of my own mind and when in saw before
My eyes Shiva and Shakti merged into one;"
Says Lalleleshwari, "And there I also won
To the Lake of immortal Bliss my way:
And while alive, unchained live from that day,
Full from the wheel of birth and death set free.
What harm can then this world do unto me."

One bubbling fountain of surpassing joy,
Spontaneous, ceaseless, pure without alloy.
Like air unseen, caresses distant coasts
And e'en rebounds across the starry hosts:
As far off cosmic masses that we see
Are not external, as they seem to be,
But all creations of the flaming Main
Of Life, of which a droplet lights the brain.

2

Most of the mystics have no secret made
Of flooding joy and rapture that invade
The soul when drawn into the ecstatic trance,
Which some ascribe to illusion, some to chance,
And by their wrong assessment often show
Their nescience of what they should better know:
That mystic state, with its unlimited joy,
Which our discordant ways of life destroy,
Is not a special gift, nor special Grace,
But an Estate designed for all the race.
And all those who possessed this matchless gift
Nature did not for special favour sift,
But by inheritance and healthy mode
Of life were able to climb up the road,

---

[1]Lal Dad Jaya Lal Kaul.

Aligned for every soul to ascend before
It to immortal heights of Bliss can soar.

Not only we, e'en scholars find it hard
To fathom those who win this rare reward,
To place themselves in mind into their shoes,
When they on mystics and their visions muse.
But some of them beguiled by pride cannot
Arrive at this conclusion in their thought,
That as an infant cannot know or guess
The thrill that follows, when two lovers press
Together, in the same way normal minds
Can ne'er imagine what a mystic finds
In his unutterable ecstatic flights
Towards the Source of all thrills and delights.

Can we conceive, whate'er the effort made,
How animals muse, what thoughts their mind pervade,
What is their picture of creation seen,
And their response or difference in between
The image of one and another class
Of quadrupeds, say of an ox and ass?
Or say the difference met between a bird
And beast, save what is fancied or inferred?

Can we e'en visualize a person's mind,
Excelling ours or of an inferior kind,
Or our own, as a child, before the dawn
Of self-awareness, as we picture brawn?

Then for the common mind where lies the chance
To draw a picture of the ecstatic trance;
A state of being so far in advance
No average mind can grasp it at a glance.
But so enthralling, full of pure romance,
That, when thus blessed, e'en ascetics sing and dance!

Where lies the scope then for the learned don
And his voluminous books to dwell upon
This most exceptional state of Consciousness,
No normal mind can picture and express,
Unless it has the experience of the state,
And gift of clear expression to relate

A rare domain impossible to describe
Howe'er rich be the words and skilled the scribe.

Those who have no experience of the trance
Can frame a distant picture if, by chance,
They have the gift to taste the aesthetic thrills,
When rapturous melody or beauty fills
The heart to cause emotions with no name
That keep us spell-bound, leaving as they came
From depths of consciousness to enchant a while
With but a handful from an endless pile;
A sample picked at random from the store
Of bliss pervading mind's transcendent shore.

That verdant meadow, mixing with its green
Sweet, little flowers of every colour seen,
Tossing high their heads in the sportive breeze
To keep time with the gently swaying trees,
As meandering in the grass the warbling stream
Intones its music to complete the dream;
While just above a gorgeous rainbow spans
The sky, descending low to watch the dance.

When nature brings together all her clan
In harmony to feast the eye of man
The effect can be so charming, wondrous, grand
As to eclipse a fancied fairy-land,
To cause the ecstacies and moods intense
When music, beauty and charm ravish sense,
Unnoticed by those distant grazing flocks
As dead to this charm as the encircling rocks.

These lovely landscapes we oft live among
Have been the pet themes of which muse has sung,
With its embellishments, to bring before
The mind their beauty, heightened all the more.
The same applies to every form of art
Which makes intense appeal to mortal heart.

The rare artistic treasures of the race,
Depict some facet of charm, beauty, grace,

Of courage, strength, peace, harmony or love,
Romance, truth, justice, faith or God above
And why? Because man's evolution tends
Towards already mapped aesthetic ends.

This racial genius during all its span
Has tried to bring before the eye of man,
In every age and nigh in every clime,
Cut to the mental stature of the time,
For at the apex of his glory man
Must be their radial-centre, if he can.

Religious genius has to grow so tall
It must ascend to heights above them all,
To bring within its sight the lofty goal
Of which rest are the oozings from one whole;
The aim and end of mystic ecstasy
Is one with the source of these drops to be!

These varied dribblets, numerous in their count
Emerge from but one inexhaustible Fount
Of bliss, called Ananda by the seers of yore,
Held to be flowing from the conscious core
Of all creation which, the more we near
The more distinct becomes this joy and cheer.

The evolution of mankind proceeds,
If we do not impede it with our deeds,
Towards a new awareness, a new cast
Of mind, so utterly joyful and so fast,
So calm and beatific and so enhanced
In wide perception of truth, when entranced
Or in perennial seers, e'en when awake,
That heaven and earth seem shadowy and fake,
Compared to this new-opened world sublime,
Beyond expression, e'er fresh, e'er in prime.

And hence the swooming rapture, thrilling joy,
For this is naked life, without alloy:
Who clothed in flesh too oft forgets herself,
And gallops after shadows—power and pelf—

But ne'er appeased or happy, as desire
Increases the more it is fed like fire.

The purple sunset and the rosy dawn
The gleaming starry sky, the spacious lawn,
The sylvian landscape or the desert wide,
The leaping waterfall and rushing tide,
The sprawling mountain, ocean's vast expanse,
Which charm the eye, expand heart, mind entrance,
With their dimension, setting, beauty, grace
Of contour, colour, feature, form or face,
Excite profound emotions—wonder, awe,
Delight and admiration—that e'en thaw
The hardest natures, often lost in thought,
How this enchanting picture has been wrought.

All these emotions—wonder, awe and joy—
Are born of virgin life, demure and coy,
Not from those prodigious masses, earth and stone,
For life can e'en create them all alone,
As grandeur, charm or colour of a scene
Lie in her, not in objects, blue or green.

In ecstasy the mystic, when in Grace,
Is brought with unattired Life face to face.
The thrilling rapture of this union, who
With apt description can convey to you,
As maiden Life this thrill has only kept
For him who steady of mind is not swept,
By curbless passion and desire, away
For Her immortal Shrine, lost in the way.

One touch, one soft caress, one fond embrace
And sorrows vanish leaving not a trace,
The sun of happiness, high up behind,
With its delightful luster fills the mind.
In this enchanting glow the cosmos wears
A beauty so sublime that it brings tears
To eyes, makes nerves tingle, senses thrill,
The hairs to stand on end, and heart to fill

With sweet emotion and deep thankfulness,
At this Divine estate of Consciousness.

Picture the great explosion if the joy
Of your life, since you found it in a toy,
Were, all combined, at once to invade your heart,
And then to all the pores of body dart,
Holding you dazed and breathless for a while,
The joy expanding like the flooded Nile.

Remember that our happiness springs
From Life, the Fount of joy, the king of kings:
The joy extracted from triumphant sport,
Victorious war, high rank, imperial court,
Unique adventure, matchless enterprise,
Distinguished scholarship with Nobel prize,
From study, honour, strength, original thought,
Exceptional talent, masterpieces wrought,
From beauty, glamour, sweet romantic love,
Fine children, consort or accomplished vow;
All comes from Life and can, with Grace Divine,
Be had in full from her exhaustless Mine.

Combine this joy of all successful lives,
Of happy husbands and delighted wives,
And you will have a picture, rather faint,
Of rapture that attends the illumined saint.
It wells from soul, the Spring-head of all bliss,
Which oft because of ignorance we miss.

3

A faint reflection of this state supreme,
A breath, a whisper, just a distant gleam,
Apart from mystics and awakened minds,
Whose life it lusters and ennobles, finds
Confirming echoes heard time after time
From gifted intellects of many a clime,

From poets, scientists, philosophers,
Expressed or hinted at in prose and verse
Which, like dispersing sparks that set on fire
Combustive stuff, touch a vibrating wire
In longing hearts and help to bring more near
The music of the Unknown they love to hear.

This is what Coleridge says:
"And what if all animated nature[1]
Be but organic harps diversely formed
That tremble into thought as ov'r them sweeps
Plastic and vast, one intellectual breeze
At once the soul of each and God of all."

And this Einstein:
"The most beautiful emotion we can
experience is the mystical. It is the source
of all true art and science. . . . To know
that what is impenetrable to us really exists,
manifesting itself as the highest wisdom
and the most radiant beauty which
our dull faculties can comprehend in their
most primitive forms—this knowledge,
this feeling is at the center of true religiousness.
In this sense and in this sense only I belong
to the ranks of devoutly religious men."

This Robert Browning:
"Truth is within ourselves; it takes no rise
From outward things, whate'er you may believe,
There is an inmost center in us all,
Where truth abides in fullness; and around
Wall upon wall, the gross flesh hems it in,
This perfect, clear perception which is truth.

A baffling and perverting carnal mesh
Blinds it, and makes all error: and to know

_____

[1]The Aeolian Harp.

Rather consists in opening out a way
Whence the imprisoned splendour may escape,
Than in effecting entry for a light
Supposed to be without."

This Sir James Jeans;
"But the physical theory of relativity has now shown[1]
that electric and magnetic forces are not real at all,
they are mere mental constructs of our own,
resulting from our rather misguided efforts to understand
the motions of the particles. It is the same
with the Newtonian force of gravitation
and with energy, momentum and other concepts
which were introduced to help us understand
the activities of the world—all prove to be
mental constructs, and do not even pass the test
of objectivity. If the materialists are pressed
to say how much of the world they now claim
as material their only possible answer
would seem to be: Matter itself. Thus their
whole philosophy is reduced to a tautology.
But the fact that so much of what used to be thought
to possess an objective physical existence
now proves to consist only of subjective
mental constructs must surely be counted
a pronounced step in the direction of mentalism.

" . . . And now that we find that we can best understand
the course of events in terms of waves
of knowledge, there is a certain presumption—
although certainly no proof—that reality
and knowledge are similar in their natures,
or, in other words, that reality is wholly mental.

Before the latter alternative can be
seriously considered, some answer must be found
to the problem of how objects can continue

---

[1]Physics and Philosophy.

to exist when they are not being perceived
in any human mind. There must, as Berkeley says, be
'some other mind in which they exist.'
Some will wish to describe this, as the mind
of God; others with Hegel as a universal
or Absolute mind in which all our individual minds
are comprised. The new quantum mechanics may perhaps
give a hint, although nothing more than
a hint, as to how this can be."

This Teilhard de Chardin:
"But even in the interest of life in general,[1]
what is the work of works for man
if not to establish, in and by each of us,
an absolutely original center in which
the universe reflects itself in a unique
and inimitable way. And these centers are
our very selves and personalities. The very center
of our consciousness, deeper than all its radii,
that is the essence which Omega, if it is
to be truly Omega, must reclaim. And this essence
is obviously not something of which we
can dispossess ourselves for the torch.
For we are the very flame of that torch.
To communicate itself, my ego must subsist
through abandoning itself or the gift will fade away.
The conclusion is inevitable that the concentration
of a conscious universe would be unthinkable
if it did not reassemble in itself all consciousnesses
as well as the conscious; each particular consciousness
remaining conscious of itself at the end of the operation,
and even (this must absolutely be understood)
each particular consciousness becoming
still more itself and thus more clearly distinct
from others the closer it gets to them in Omega."

---

[1]The Phenomenon of Man.

This Jami:
"The Loved One's rose-parterre I went to see,[1]
That beauty's Torch espied me, and, quoth He,
'I am the tree, these flowers my offshoots are,
Let not these offshoots hide from thee the tree.

What profit rosy cheeks, forms full of grace,
And ringlets clustering round a lovely face?
When Beauty Absolute beams all around
Why linger finite beauties to embrace?'"

This Emerson:
"Meantime within man is the soul of the whole[2]
the wise silence; the universal beauty,
to which every part and particle is equally related;
the eternal One. And this deep power in which we exist
and whose beatitude is all accessible to us,
is not only self-sufficing and perfect in every hour,
but the act of seeing and the thing seen, the seer
and the spectacle, the subject and the object are one.
We see the world piece by piece, as the sun,
the moon, the animal, the tree; but the whole, of which
these are the shining parts, is the soul.
. . . My words do not carry its august sense;
they fall short and cold. Only itself can inspire
whom it will, and behold! Their speech
shall be lyrical, and sweet, and universal
as the rising of the wind. Yet I desire,
even by profane words, if I may not use sacred,
to indicate the heaven of this deity
and to report what hints I have collected
of the transcendent simplicity
and energy of the Highest Law."

This Shelley:
"The Light whose smile kindles the universe,

---

[1]Jami, translated by E. H. Whinfield.
[2]The Over-Soul.

93

That Beauty in which all things work and move,
That Benediction which the eclipsing curse
Of birth can quench not, that sustaining Love
Which through the web of being blindly wove
By man and beast and earth and air and sea,
Burns bright or dim, as each are the mirrors of
The fire for which all thirst . . ."

This A.S. Eddington:
". . . The leading points which have seemed [1]
to me to deserve philosophical consideration
may be summarized as follows:

(1) The symbolic nature of the entities
of physics is generally recognized, and the scheme
of physics is now formulated in such a way
as to make it self-evident that it is
a partial aspect of something wider.

(2) Strict causality is abandoned in
the material world. Our ideas of the controlling laws
are in process of reconstruction and it is
not possible to predict what kind of form
they will ultimately take; but all the indications are
that strict causality has dropped out permanently.
This relieves the former necessity of supposing
that mind is subject to deterministic law
or alternatively that it can suspend
deterministic law in the material world.

(3) Recognizing that the physical world
is entirely abstract and without 'actuality'
apart from its linkage to consciousness,
we restore consciousness to the fundamental position
instead of representing it as an inessential complication
occasionally found in the midst of inorganic nature
at a late stage of evolutionary history.

_____

[1]The Nature of the Physical World.

94

(4) The sanction for correlating a 'real' physical world
to certain feelings of which we are conscious
does not seem to differ in any essential respect
from the sanction for correlating a spiritual domain
to another side of our personality."

This Plato:
"The man who has been guided thus far[1]
in the mysteries of love, and who has directed
his thought towards examples of beauty in due
and orderly succession, will suddenly have
revealed to him as he approaches the end
of his initiation a beauty whose nature
is marvellous indeed, the final goal, Socrates,
of all his previous efforts. This beauty
is first of all eternal, it neither comes into being
nor passes away, neither waxes nor wanes;
next, it is not beautiful in part and ugly
in part, not beautiful at one time and ugly
at another, nor beautiful in this relation
and ugly in that, nor beautiful here
and ugly there, as varying according
to the beholders; nor again will this beauty
appear to him like the beauty of a face
or hands or anything else corporeal,
or like the beauty of a thought or a science,
or like the beauty which has its seat
in something other than itself, be it
a living thing or the earth or the sky
or anything else whatever; he will see it
as absolute, existing alone with itself,
unique, eternal, and all other beautiful things
as partaking of it, yet in such a manner
that, while they come into being and pass away,
it neither undergoes any increase
or diminution or suffers any change."

[1]The Symposium.

This Wordsworth:
". . . something far more deeply interfused,
Whose dwelling place is the light of setting suns
And the round ocean, and the living air,
And the blue sky, and in the mind of man;
A motion and a spirit, that impels
All thinking things, all objects of all thought,
And rolls through all things."

This John Ruskin:
"Lastly, although there was no definite[1]
religious sentiment mingled with it, there was
a continual perception of Sanctity
in the whole of nature from the slightest thing
to the vastest; an instinctive awe, mixed with delight;
an indefinable thrill, such as we sometimes imagine
to indicate the presence of a disembodied spirit.
I could only feel this perfectly when I was alone,
and then it would often make me shiver from head
to foot with the joy and fear of it . . . . These
feelings remained in their full intensity
till I was eighteen or twenty and then,
as the reflective and practical power increased
and the cares of the world gained upon me,
faded gradually away, in the manner described
by Wordsworth in his 'Intimations of Immortality.' "

This John Mansfield:
"The station brook to my new eyes[2]
Was babbling out of paradise,
The waters rushing from the rain
Were singing Christ is risen again,
I thought all earthly creatures knelt
For rapture of the joy I felt,
The narrow station wall's brick ledge,
The wild hop withering in the hedge,

---

[1]Modern Painters.
[2]The Everlasting Mercy.

The lights in huntsman's upper story
Were parts of an eternal glory."

Do not these few excerpts suffice to prove
That life is far more than the tiny groove
Of self and that an ocean lies behind
The individual droplet of our mind?
That men and women of high intellect
Or talent sometimes did and can detect
With logic, study or in solemn moods
The Glory which o'er all creation broods?

How well these frank expressions signify
That knowledge,·wisdom, music, beauty lie
In Life in one eternal Symphony
Which plays in muffled tones in you and me?
A new world open in us which the beast
Can ne'er attain to share the aesthetic feast,
And now, with one step gained, where lies the hitch
In what I hold out, that a still more rich
And wondrous life is possible, if we press
Into the Cosmic plane of consciousness?

4

Whate'er in all that we observe appears
Amazing, wondrous, marvellous or rare,
Or when a spectacle or object wears
Beauty or symmetry beyond compare,
Remember that you see a borrowed dress
Lent for the while to it by consciousness.

The vast dimension of the world we see
Which o'er-awes us with its immensity,
The staggering distances which light would take,
With all its dizzy speed, a round to make,
Billions of years across the enormous span,
Computed by the standards set by man,

And such a vast duration that our scale
Of measurement and mathematics fail,
Are our creations spelt in human terms,
Of what our mind about the Cosmos learns.

And e'en this process of extending wide
Our knowledge of the world, if we decide
Or judge it rationally, is not to find
Some thing external, but within our mind.
An inside drama is projected out
By some device we nothing know about.

What we deduce sometimes is pure surmise
Which true one day the next we must revise,
To keep pace with new facts that come to light
With better instruments to aid our sight,
Or better methods for the study done
By thousands of observers one by one.
Again to fish out from the boundless main
Of mind some fresh pearls by applying the brain.

The constellations, galaxies and clouds
Of nebular dust among the starry crowds,
The quasars, pulsars, comets, holes in space
And other wonders which now grow apace,
As more and more observing minds apply
Themselves to a study of the evening sky,
Borrow their measure, size, duration, mass,
Their shape and form, as they diurnally pass
Before the vision of the astronomer,
From his own mind which only can confer
The amazing properties that make the skies
A book of joy and wonder for the wise.

But more amazing than the luminous host
That greets our vision from the starry coast,
At which we look at night with eager eyes
To know what mystery behind it lies,
Is our incredible apathy towards
The Wonder from which spring these shining worlds.

The Wonder of our consciousness which we
Neglect to explore in depth, although we see
That it and it alone provides the cast
That makes the universe so huge and vast,
That it and it alone supplies the base
For all the immensity of time and space,
That it and it alone allots the size,
The shape and form which we mark with our eyes,
Also the number, distance and the span
Of time we try to calculate and scan.

Divested of the wondrous vesture lent
By consciousness to star-lit firmanent,
It is not hard to envision what is left,
If anything at all, will be bereft
Of all the exciting features—form and size,
Distance and time which from the mind arise.
And all alluring qualities will cease,
And with that our emotions too would freeze.

Will not the bright, star-spangled sky then sink
Into oblivion with no star to wink,
Causing our whole astronomy to shrink
To Zero of which we e'en cannot think?
Our study of the stars, in fact, implies
Whate'er the knowledge gathered of the skies,
For which apparently we space explore,
The plumbing of our own mind more and more.

Can we refuse to own that when we probe
The glowing sky at night it wears a robe
Of staggering breadth and mind-bewildering length,
Of vastness, fineness, density or strength,
Of wondrous workmanship, and grand design,
Not that it has on it the slightest sign
Of such a garment, but because our mind
Invests it with the features which we find
So fascinating and so marvellous
That they excite, amaze and stagger us.

We have to admit then that when we explore
The sky, or o'er the gathered data pore,
We dig at something present in our mind
Which, to come out, needs prodding of some kind,
And our astronomical study pokes
A smouldering fire which, lighted up, evokes
The images and feelings that combined
Reveal a depth profound of our own mind,
In course of time, with further prodding done,
Which may expand it more until the Sun
Of Cosmic Consciousness begins to shine
To show creation one with Life Divine.

The raw mind of the savage had no room
For such a glowing intellectual bloom,
Nor such imagery nor emotional feasts,
Nor they exist in idiots nor in beasts,
Nor e'en in sundry common minds in whom
Their own mundane affairs take all the room,
And who look at one with a vacant stare
Who knowledge of the stars would like to share
With them, much more concerned, than moons and stars,
With their own business, office, goods and cars.

It is hard to believe that consciousness,
We so neglect and talk about so less,
Is in reality the Sovereign Queen
Of all observing minds and objects seen.
Because, a natural gift, we sacrifice
Nor time nor labour nor pay any price
For its possession, treating it so cheap
That what I say may seem like a wild leap
Into the realms of myth and fantasy,
Without appeal to those who fail to see
That e'en their hyper-critical frame of mind
Flows from the spring of consciousness behind.

But their own logic contradicts amain
What they contend, for after death the brain

While still fresh and materially intact
Refuses to register and react
To sensory impressions that had lit
The glowing flame of fancy, thought and wit:
The flame which lighting up the world without
Itself remains unlighted, wrapped in doubt.

Who knows the objective world which it creates,
With all its storms and stresses, loves and hates,
Might be a training ground for it to unfold
Its majesty and gradually to mould
Itself into the Mighty Being who,
So frail and puny now in me and you,
Might grow in stature to become a god:
A Superman born of the earthly sod,
Who will have in himself discovered the Source
Of all the Wonders of the universe.

We live and grow to childhood, youth and prime,
Meet age and death, caught in the flow of time,
A dream, a fantasy, a drama played
By consciousness which sees itself arrayed
In flesh, cast on a mighty floating globe
With others, all dressed in a similar robe,
To toil and sweat, to struggle, hate and love,
Deluded always by an elusive Now;
The junction-point between receding past
And nearing future, always o'er too fast,
To experience all things in a causal chain
Which, once passed by, are ne'er the same again,
So that the experience at the end remains
Only a memory in the human brains,
A dream-like image of all past events,
Which, when recalled in retrospect, presents
A mental drama ending in a flash,
A whole life of experience turned to ash.

Where lies the wisdom, when we know before
The end of life is so distressfully sore,
So filled with vain regrets, so full of pain,
When limbs and senses trick the enfeebled brain,

In hankering after power or hoarding wealth,
With sullied conscience and depleted health?
When from one's nerve-less fingers, at the top
Of one's career, all he has won can drop,
To sigh and sorrow for the vigour past,
During the days which, he knows, are the last.

Since man can ne'er escape decay and death
Nor hold from breaking loose the imprisoned breath,
Would you prefer to enforce the dismal end,
Without exception, on those who pretend
To be the cream of the world and, when young,
Like lions, boldly plough their way among
The less astute to snatch whate'er they find
To satisfy the burning itch of mind?
Or would you choose, before the senses drown
In decadence and death, the eternal crown
Of Life Divine, to rise beyond the fears
Of mortal life, beyond its sighs and tears,
Into a higher sphere of consciousness
Where thorny problems of earth cease to press?

The gracious aim of nature is to extend
Our mind, with structural changes to that end,
Towards a new awareness, so remote
From what it is now that we cannot quote
A parallel, to make one understand
In what Elysian havens man would land,
To lead a glorious life, both in and out,
A cosmic-conscious angel sure about
His own immortal crown, surrounded by
All goods and needs of life earth can supply,
A heaven of peace and happiness around,
Where lust for power and wealth has lost all ground,
Supplanted by a more rewarding race
For exploration of the inner space!

If you desire to know, without mistake,
What true enlightenment means you should slake
Your thirst by study of the brief accounts,
Left by the Indian seers whose bubbling founts

Of cosmic-consciousness, express in words
That have out-lived the empires built with swords,
The wonder and glory of the soul,
They named Atma—the mirror of the Whole.

When the doors of perception open wide
To show the Eternal Presence which they hide,
A new internal world opens to our gaze
Of Being, Consciousness and Bliss ablaze
With Living Splendour, those enlightened seers
As Brahman named, the origin of all,
The largest and the infinitely small,
The Life of Lives and Light of Lights which shines
As lifeless matter, life in mortal shrines
And as resplendence spread all o'er the sky
In twinkling stars which greets the human eye,
And both as one and many, whole and part,
When shining in the mirror of the heart,
In every individual soul which seems
To bring to rich fulfilment all its dreams!

Pore o'er their words, and see how every one
Of them when lighted by the Eternal Sun
Of life, lost in the wonder of the soul,
Free of duality of part and whole,
In unambiguous words announced his claim
Of oneness with the all-embracing Flame.

With Brahman, Shiva, Vishnu, Ishvara,
The immortal Fount of Life from which we draw
Our being, for a while to strut and dance,
Like puppets, pulled with strings of Fate or Chance,
To act as rulers, generals, scholars, priests,
Toilers and e'en as criminals, worse than beasts,
In every garb but one Eternal Soul,
Itself the Start, the Journey and the Goal,
In countless actions playing every part,
Forgetful, such is his illusive art,
Of His Divine Estate in mortal man,
Enfleshed to solve the Riddle, when he can.

Enlightenment tears off the invisible veil
Of mass illusion, which we often fail
To notice e'en, and, as sleep-walkers lack
The knowledge of their state till they come back
To normal, that they had forgot their own
Name and identity which so well known
In wakefullness they could not now recall,
We too surrounded by the invisible wall
Of senses, only smell, touch, hear and see
What lies within their strait periphery.

The Soul hemmed in by senses is shut out
From that ubiquitous Presence, which without
The attributes that they essentially need
For its detection, lies unseen to breed
Doubts and confusion in the intellect
Which ne'er can overcome this grave defect,
If for milleniums scholars try their strength
To explore the universe in all its length,
Unless Enlightenment is sought to teach
What otherwise must lie beyond their reach.

5

I could mistrust my judgment if it were
A matter of a day, when far and near
A glorious Immanence delights my eyes,
As if the sun descending from the skies
On earth, become a living radiance, bathes
All objects in a lustre which ne'er fades,
Lending to the surroundings such a charm
That they of all unrest the mind disarm.

But now since thirty years I see and hear
What is so distant from our normal sphere
Of life, so stunning, so amazing, rare
That, though enjoying it, I hardly dare
Believe that earth can offer such a balm,
Become such an abode of bliss and calm,

That e'en the fabulous charms of Eden seem
No more substantial than a wishful dream
Before the stark reality of this
Objective life of blessedness, peace and bliss.

So ineffable and so hard to paint
In words that all I say would be too faint
To draw a picture of this gift sublime,
E'en if I try my best in prose and rhyme
To express the marvels which I see and hear,
Abounding all around me, so I fear
That e'en the most exact account I write
Can ne'er do justice to the glorious sight,
Which nature has reserved man's eye to charm,
His mind to broaden and his heart to warm,
When, keeping his life from excesses free,
He learns to activate Kundalini.

What I have gained I honestly believe
A thousand seekers can with ease achieve
Today, already when the mind of man
Has gained in stature and increased in span,
And is ripe, at least in the more advanced
And more intelligent ones to taste, entranced,
The rapture of communion with the soul,
Not by withdrawing into a lonely hole,
Nor by renouncing every joy of life,
Nor by abstaining from one's bounden strife,
But with intelligent hold on thought and deed
By following the mode of life we need
To further nature's effort to exalt
Us to Seraphic rank, to reach the vault
Of heaven, united with the Cosmic Stream
Of Life more joyful than our happiest dream.

For every visionary experience gained,
Whate'er its form, by whomsoe'er attained,
The one criterion to access its worth .
Is: it should not resemble aught of earth,
Because enlightened consciousness implies
A Plane of Being ne'er perceived with eyes

Nor other senses, so strange it defies
Description, though in all things yet aloof,
So clear and manifest it needs no proof,
Yet so elusive one can never catch
Its firm reflection or find aught to match;
A mystery so awful and so deep
Yet so alluring and sweet it can keep
The mind engrossed with such entrancing grip
No luscious Venus pressing lip to lip
Can reach, a wonder that can never cease
A joy that ne'er does lessen but increase.

When I seek to depict this wondrous state
I take due care not to exaggerate,
Nor add a single word I feel would make
A strictly true description partly fake,
Avoid those glowing narratives that are
The themes of those no scruple make to mar
The bloom of life of many credulous souls
And make them search towns, wildernesses and holes,
Himalayan snow caps, valleys, chasms and clefts
For fabulous masters, yogis and adepts,
Alleged to have such power o'er life and death,
They can enlighten one with but a breath,
Confer miraculous gifts or with a glance
Of grace induce the illumining Yoga-trance.

Had nature secret back doors to her plans
That could reduce what needs hard, lengthy spans
Of time to accomplish to a single glance
Of favour of a master, met by chance,
Then all his trials of a million years,
Which moistened earth with man's sweat, blood and tears
Could be avoided if there were a way
To circumvent the laws his Fate now sway.
Why then should millions e'en in this bright age
Remain uncured if there were but one sage
Who could devise a safe miraculous cure
Of but one ailment in most cases sure?

Though psychical displays and psychic cures
Are witnessed every day but none ensures
A constant, at-will demonstrable gift
Which could bring peace or mentally uplift,
Or light one's inner being too to place
A treasure into the hands of the race.
But on the other hand all that we see
Are weird occurrences still a mystery,
As dark yet as in the forgotten time
When glamorous Pharaohs had shone in their prime.

How can we help one for whom Fate has ruled
By his own wrong belief to live befooled?
The greatest emphasis of Faith has been
Upon a life harmonious, good and clean,
Unselfish with trust in the power above,
Of charity, compassion, truth and love,
With promise of salvation for the soul
And hope of union with God, as the whole
Reward for life-long hard endeavour done
For righteous acts performed and kudos won.

But not a word to exhaust one's energy
In running after, like a darting bee,
Clairvoyant gifts or supernatural boons
Which too keep souls imprisoned like cocoons,
For if enlightenment means magical gift
Then it can but confuse and ne'er uplift.

The reason for the current frantic rush
For magic and the occult which tend to crush
The spark of self-reforming zeal in man—
That is why Faith had put them under ban—
Is that in general we are lacking in
The knowledge of the Royal Guest within,
Attired in flesh who, now in you and me,
Forgetful of His rank and Majesty,
Identifies himself with body and
His kith and kin, His home and native land,
Waiting for us to open one more door
In our corporeal frame for him to soar

To realms of glory his eternal home,
As high and boundless as the starry dome.

We still are not aware what treasure lies
In us and what imprisoned glory tries
To free itself to make our life sublime,
And help our mind attain a golden prime,
Before which all our thoughts of greatness fade
Into oblivion, for we now are made
Conscious of what we ne'er could know before:
Eternal Life alive in every pore;

A state of blessedness momently which brings
Such joy and fullness that e'en mighty kings
Could ne'er dream of, since till the parting breath
They ne'er could drive away the fear of death:
A state of calm and beatitude which lasts
Through all vicissitudes, denials and fasts
Unto the end, and makes the life of man
One long Elysian spring for all the span
Of his terrestrial stay, at last to part
Awake to his Divinity at heart.

What can match this fulfilling life of bliss
That, once attained, no one would like to miss
For all the wealth of earth or all the seats
Of power or talent for miraculous feats,
Which, like deceptive shadows gone at night,
Depart abruptly when death comes in sight
To leave their owners who had battled long,
Betrayed their comrades or done other wrong,
For their sake, trembling and dismayed before
The awful darkness of the other shore.

Had we the slightest clue to our high state,
Our glorious empire and divine estate
Which we have lost, but can regain with ease,
If we excesses and pretensions cease,
Do you think once this sovereign goal is proved,
Beyond doubt, people will remain unmoved

At the stupendous prospect and persist
In such aims and objectives that resist
This natural trend from moulding us apace,
Among Immortals to deserve a place,
To taste, while still incarnate, that rare wine
Of Everlasting Life and Love Divine,
Each drop whereof becomes an ocean which,
Curing the mind of every lustful itch,
Keeps it serene and happy, rapt within
In Melodies Divine that keep off sin.

We do not know the Goal nor e'en the Way
To it: the worst misfortune of our day,
And lost like children in a trackless wood
Have yet to find what course for us is good.
How to deport ourselves and plan our lives,
Our households, institutions, business hives,
In consonance with our inherent trends,
Our golden prospects and exalted ends,
Which nature promises if we make a drive,
For them, while still young, healthy and alive
In all our faculties, to win by grace
That hard-to-parallel, distinguished place
Than which celestials have no higher crown,
Higher than highest honour, rank, renown
Which mortal man, so swayed by greed today,
Shall wear as god on earth for long to stay.

Entangled in sharp intellectual thorns
Of doubt, converting all our eves and morns
That could resemble heaven in bliss and calm,
Into a hectic world of sin and sham,
The rich and poor alike, allured by dreams
Of power, position or wealth go to extremes
Which nature's lofty purpose bring to naught
Caught in the brambles of ambitious thought,
To foul the holy breath that could transform,
From an abode of suffering, stress and storm
The world and their own selves, to live a life
Of such celestial joy, devoid of strife,

That e'en the most romantic tales which catch
Our fancy, it cannot remotely match.

They ask me oftentimes how do I have
Such firm conviction that my word will pave
The way to mass-upheavals which will bring
The world round to the state of which I sing
And I, as many times, repeat the plea
That it does not depend on them or me;
But with an insight gained by Grace Divine,
And not by any clever guess of mine,
I know the time has come to effect the change
And Heaven will matters in a way arrange
That of her own choice mankind shall create
The climate for the change, ordained by Fate.

The sudden shortage, by a political ruse,
Of but one article of common use,
I mean petroleum, has caused an uproar,
A ferment and a stir from shore to shore,
Which those who witness now its wide effect
Failed to foresee in time with intellect,
For they would ne'er be taken by surprise
Could they foreshadow it or e'en surmise.

But wise now after the event some try
To use to profit e'en this hue and cry,
While others sobered by a sense of guilt,
On what a weak base human life is built,
Declare we should live in a simpler way
And take to heart the lesson of today.

One single crisis, not at all so grave
To endanger life and make it hard to save,
Has sown the seeds of change in human thought,
And, e'en if this change at once is not wrought,
It has in motion set a rippling wave
In minds, to it one day the way shall pave.

We seldom realize, so prone are we
To be deceived by what we round us see,

That nature in one moment can efface
Or e'en accomplish what can take the race
A nation or a group an age to achieve,
And with one unexpected coup can leave
In utter want those who in millions roll
Or magnates make of those who live on dole,
When it her purpose suits and this applies
To changes, I foresee, of global size.

Before the very eyes of those who scoff
At warning signs, a day, not now far off,
Shall come to bring down hurtling round our ears
The structures, we have built wth blood and tears,
To install new orders, values, goals and aims
Of which we do not know yet e'en the names,
To bring about a universal change
In human life, of such extended range
That our own progeny shall view with shame
The battlefield we civilization name.

Nothing will stop the Almighty Cosmic Main
Of life, behind the evolving human brain,
To bring about the social changes sought
To extend the area of human thought,
And open fresh horizons that can bring
Into the mind of man a blooming spring
Of new ideas, ambitions, hopes and dreams,
Where now a cut-throat strife ideal seems.

A drastic change to do away with all
The false chimeras that keep us in thrall,
Replacing greed for power, possession, wealth
With aims that add to virtue, joy and health,
Which can be feasible only when the urge,
Subconscious now, for change effects a purge
With an upheaval global in extent
To effect renewals in our life and bent
Of mind, upholding o'er our present aims,
Ignoble methods and unworthy games,
The chaste endeavour for our destined goal
To unveil and share the glory of the soul.

Despite the buffets I received from Fate
For lack of clue to my precarious state,
And doubt about the mighty force I stirred
To activity, despite the risks incurred,
The errors made and the suspense I bore,
Despite the hammering that my system wore,
I still emerged with all my strength intact,
More balanced than before in thought and act,
More talented, discerning, skilled with pen,
More humble with the picture in my ken
Of my short-comings ere the power awoke,
Refashioned me and my resistence broke.

And still with all the pounding, strain and stress,
Omissions and defaults I won access
To a Kingdom I could ne'er dream of before,
Which gains in power and beauty more and more,
Such that it makes me wonder many a time
What further marvels will attend its prime,
Carrying the rapture e'en into my dreams,
So that with every breath to me it seems
I live in Paradise on earth, with heart
Melting in gratitude, to do my part.

4
THE WAY
TO ENLIGHTENMENT

1

There is but one Way, one eternal Path,
But one Direction, one ambrosial Bath
For self-unfoldment, one immutable Law
That only can us to self-knowledge draw:
One precious kernel, one essential seed,
Found in the scriptures of each major creed:
The basic teaching of all current faiths
Which our whole-hearted compliance still awaits.

The flaw has been we to the skies extolled
The Founders of our Faiths and proud installed
Their idols, relics, pictures and the rest,
Their gospels and their thought, not in our breast,
But in palatial temples, churches, shrines,
Of stately looks and masterly designs,
To quench our thirst for pomp, and tried our best
To exalt them over others and invest

Their persons and their words with such a bright
And supernatural halo that the Light
They came to shed remained confined within
The walls of sanctums they were worshipped in.

Or in the homage shown to their great works,
Their interpreters and their priestly clerks,
All hoping to obtain a modest share
Of glory if they, with assiduous care,
Applauded their own faith above the rest,
To fail deplorably in the first test
To treat the others like one'self to trace
A most essential guideline for the race.

But where the seeds had to be deeply sown
Remained as barren as if hewn of stone:
The human heart which had to study, sift
And act upon the precepts in their gift,
To reach the state sublime they promised all
Those who might rally to their clarion call.

Instead of striving for a study deep
And critical we turned into docile sheep
Their followers, contending that their words
Contained the wisdom found in all the worlds,
With this fanatical, religious zeal
We narrowed down and put a binding seal
On the revealed injunctions but to feed
Our vanity and not to advance the creed.

For what the Founders said remained unchanged
By praise or criticism, but we deranged
Our thinking, when we chose to shut our eyes
To the truth that there is more in the skies
And on the earth than mortal mind can know,
Whereof the admission spurs us on to grow,
While by assuming that there is no more
To learn, on knowledge we tight shut the door.

That is why nature to remove the clamp
That had constricted human thought to cramp

The growth of knowledge which could not but stunt
Our mind, arrayed a formidable front
Of powerful intellects in Europe who
Remorselessly, as if dispatched to do
The task, the sovereignty of Faith dethroned,
Attacked her sanctum, battered it and stoned,
And left her flat to learn with pain and smart
That all our scriptures augur but the start
Of long, adventurous journeys that shall last
Until mankind to the earth can hold fast,
Beginning from a few, to win with Grace
The glorious empire of Self for the race.

The tendency in modern intellects
To expose the fallacies, faults and defects
In sacred teachings fails to take account
Of the plain fact that masses cannot mount
As fast the heights of thought that are innate
In them, and hence in their immature state
Of mind it is a grave mistake to uproot
Their faith and cause digression from the Route.

In rituals, ceremonies and pomp was lost
The teaching which, beyond compare and cost,
Terrestrial consciousness revealed to man
To draw his first attention to the Plan:
To curb the passions human nature bind
And labour for a cosmic-conscious mind,
Which soaring from the carnal nest could reach
Eternal Life the prophets came to preach
In stories, parables, allegories,
Aphorisms, sermons and mythologies
To suit the measure of the intellect
Of average mortals, not but the elect,
For revelation comes to guide the mass
Of mankind, not but those the crowd surpass.

What I assert can be seen e'en today
With but a little thought and brief survey:
Is rationalist approach to faith the rage
Of people e'en in this enlightened age?

115

Or more than e'er they are invaded by
Irrational impulses, which probe defy?

Or do they stop to reason when they run
After a mountebank or any one
Known for miraculous power or saintliness,
And do they not soon crowd round him and press,
All eager for some boon or gift of grace?
If not obliged do they not run apace
To others, loath to disabuse their minds
Of the lure of the uncanny which oft binds
The thought of man to be refined and used
To profit, when the true Light is diffused?

In pre-Renaissance days did we have more
Of myth and superstition than the store
Unev'nly shared by present-day mankind?
And do we not an equal measure find
Of faith in magic, witch-craft, sorcery,
Sooth-saying and the occult from what we see
Today, when hundreds of books in a year,
To bits which common-sense and reason tear,
Are read by millions so avidly with
The firm conviction they are not a myth?

Some as fantastic as Gulliver's Tales:
Of human beings of the size of nails,
Tales of adepts, magicians, sorcerers,
Tibetan Lamas or Himalayan seers,
Brazilian wizards or some other freaks,
Who can bestow whate'er the boon one seeks,
Not met in flesh, save in the inventive mind
Of those such fantasies of profit find.

Is not there as keen interest, as much faith
In spirit, demon, poltergeist and wraith,
In mediums and in psi-phenomena?
The products of a still unfathomed law,
Of which none e'er could make the head or tail
And e'en the most astute observers fail

To find the agent or locate the force,
Delighting in such weird, bizarre and coarse
Displays, but still no rhyme nor reason find
For this irrational frolic of our mind,
That makes none happier, wiser, more serene;
Is just a mystery and so has been
And so shall be until we learn the laws
Which of religious genius are the cause.

These Laws of Life none can reveal save Faith—
Idle to expect this from a ghost or wraith—
And that is what the Enlightened came to teach:
The primary steps for us the height to reach,
And that is why a riot has begun
With hundreds of new cults instead of one:
Why hundreds of new prophets in the field
Their poverty with loud drum-beating shield.
And that is why these teeming mushroom cults
All o'er the earth produce such poor results
That we have not progressed a furlong more
Than where we were three thousand years before.

All that the founders of these movements tell
The same old wine they in new bottles sell,
For were there something new in their discourse
It would provide a strong cementing force,
Our greatest need, not a divisive one
Which some accept, some spurn, some treat as fun.

Instead of stressing where their greatness lay,
Their deep sincerity and selfless way
Of life, superb example and high thought,
Their strength and wisdom which upheavals wrought,
We turned our prophets into deities who
Nothing in common had with me or you.
Who had not battled and essayed for long
To turn their mind from passion, sin and wrong,
Who were above the reach of carnal love
And e'en in fancy never broke the vow,

Above all faults and blemishes which make,
As they are handled, mortals gold or fake,
And which, a common feature of their life,
Demand an honest and heroic strife,
Decreed by nature, as part of the Plan
For the ennoblement and rise of man.

How could the laity emulate with zeal
Their great example when thus made to feel
Inferior beings meant to obey the writ,
Whate'er their wisdom, courage, strength and grit,
And ne'er to dream that they could also rise,
With effort, at least, to approximate size?
The natural target for the human race
Lost in the battle for the pride of place!

Where lies the difference 'twixt a hard endeavour
For ecclesiastic or temporal power,
Whether a palace is built for a king
Or an imposing shrine for crowds to sing
Hymns of praise to the Lord or if we raise
The Enlightened too to power with fulsome praise,
Rather than treat them as compassionate guides
To lead us to the place where Truth resides,
And let not our temporal thirsts replace
The gratitude to be shown in this case.

The Founders of our faiths, revered and praised,
Always austere and humble, never raised,
Luxurious mansions for themselves or God,
Preached in the open, sat and slept on sod
Sheltered by trees, embracing rich and poor,
The high and low to make their mission sure.

How can then present-day religions win
The hearts of men, when they are void within
Of what their Founders spared no pains to instill:
A moderate, honest way of life to will
And gain salvation for the embodied soul,
Of Knowledge and Religion the one Goal,

The one supreme objective of our life,
The ground for all our sweating toil and strife,
The reason why we are and why we came,
The baffling mystery behind the game;
Our precious soul—a deathless spark divine
Of Cosmic Life—must in his glory shine.

There is no difference in what I declare
And in the basic tenets, we all share,
Of every major faith and every creed
In which revealed directions came to lead
The straggling human flock to its estate,
Free of aggression, envy, malice, hate,
Unbridled lust, ambition, thirst for power,
The cause of chaos we see at this hour,
For they oppose the Laws which rule the pace
Of man's evolving brain in time and space.

So all the Anointed in their time bespoke
The perils that await unwary folk,
If they continue to infringe the Law,
And they too listened with respect and awe,
Instinctively aware from olden time
That oracles can tell in prose and rhyme
What future holds, and though sometimes abused,
The gift of presage cannot be refused
Acceptance, and this is where science erred
And into a scorpion pit all mankind hurled.

A temperate life, awareness of the Goal,
Reflection, meditation, self-control,
A noble way of conduct, thought and deed,
The basic virtues taught in every creed,
Contentment, rectitude, compassion, love,
Altruism as much as one's means allow,
No dogma, no self-torture, no extreme
Are steps that lead toward the Light supreme.

This is the way to accelerate the pace
Of both the individual and the race

Towards the Target; but now out of tune
The race is threatened with upheaval soon,
To exact submission to the unwritten Law
And clean the human mind of filth and straw,
Which now appear alluring, to replace
Them with a nobler hunger in the race
For peace, eternal life and love divine
With joy untold to fill each mortal shrine.

2

Nature in all exigencies upholds
The Law which mortal brain and body moulds,
And this is why revealed instructions came
At crucial times to light the intuitive Flame,
That can illuminate the hidden Path
To avoid slips and a serious aftermath.

But oft unmindful of the noble aim
For which religions and their Founders came,
More than the crowds, those who professed to be
The orbs of Light and holders of the key
To theophanic mysteries construed
The Message as they liked and oft pursued
A path discordant with the teachings left,
The same in all creeds in their warp and weft.

Lost in lip-service rites and loud acclaim
We grew indifferent to the lofty aim
Of Holy Writs and their stress on the need
To help, with due restraint in thought and deed,
The evolutionary processes at work,
In every human being, Frank or Turk,
To win the prize which all the Illumined name:
Union with its Source for the incarnate Flame
Of Life: the vision of its glorious state
To which man has to grow up soon or late.

It is remarkable most prophets chose
To name their doctrines as a Path for those
Who, with belief in them, would like to share
A paradise rich with enchanting ware,
A heavenly kingdom or Nirvanic joy,
Brahmanic peace and bliss which never cloy,
In every case a glorious, happy goal,
The eternal splendent empire of the soul.

This is what Gita says:
"Whate'er the Path pursued by men to attain[1]
To me by that identical path they gain
My favour, Arjuna (wherev'r they bide)
Men follow but my path from every side."

And again:
"This Yoga handed down from sire to son,
Arjuna, known to many an illumined one,
The royal sages, by great efflux of time,
Has disappeared more or less (from our clime).
This same perennial Yoga I impart
To you today because you are at heart
My devotee and friend and so I deem
You fit to share this secret lore supreme."

This from Christ:
"I am come a light into the world."[2]
"That whosoever believeth on me should not
 abide in darkness."
"And if any man hear my words and believe not
I judge him not: for I came not to judge
the world, but to save the world . . . .
For I have not spoken of myself; but the Father
which sent me, he gave me a commandment,
What I should say and what I should speak.
And I know that this commandment is life everlasting:

---

[1]Bhagwad Gita IV. 2, 3.
[2]John 12, 46-47, 49-50.

Whatsoever I speak therefore, even as the father
said unto me, so I speak."

Again:
"Ye are the light of the world. A city[1]
that is set on a hill cannot be hid.
Neither do men light a candle and put it
under a bushel, but on a candlestick;
and it gives light unto all that
are in the house.
Let your light so shine before men, that they
may see your good works, and glorify
your Father which is in heaven.
Think not that I am come to destroy the law
or the prophets: I am not come to destroy
but to fulfil.
For verily I say unto you, till heaven
and earth pass, one jot or one tittle
shall in no wise pass from the law,
till all be fulfilled."

Again:
"Sanctify them through thy truth:[2]
thy word is truth.
As thou hast sent me into the world,
even so have I also sent them into the world.
And for their sakes I sanctify myself,
that they may also be sanctified
through the truth.
Neither pray I for these alone,
But for them also which shall believe
on me through their word;
That they all may be one; as thou, Father,
art in me, and I in thee, that they also
may be one in us: that the world
may believe that thou hast sent me.

[1]Matthew 5, 14-18
[2]John 17, 17-23

And the glory which thou gavest me
I have given them, that they may be one
even as we are one:
I in them and thou in me, that they may
be made perfect in one; and that the world
may know that thou hast sent me,
and hast loved them, as thou hast loved me."

This from Buddha:
"Even so have I, monks, seen an ancient way[1]
an ancient road followed by
the wholly awakened ones of olden times . . . .
Along that have I gone and the matters
that I have come to know fully as I was
going along it, I have told to the monks,
nuns, men and women lay-followers. Let,
Monks, this Brahma-faring that is prosperous
and flourishing, wide-spread and widely known
become popular—in short, well made manifest
for Devas and men."

Again:
"It may be, Ananda, that some of you will think:[2]
The word of the teacher is ended; we have no teacher.
But it is not to be regarded in this way.
That Dhamma and discipline taught and laid down
by me, this is to be your teacher after my passing on.
Come now, monks, all component things
are liable to decay, call up diligence
to accomplish your aim."

Again:
"The Tathagata does not seek salvation[3]
in austerities, but neither does he
for that reason indulge in worldly pleasures,

---

[1]Samyutta Nikaya
[2]Dhiga Nikaya
[3]Mahavagga

nor live in abundance. The Tathagata
has found the middle path."

"There are two extremes, O Bhikkhus,
which the man who has given up the world
ought not to follow—the habitual practice,
on the one hand, of self-indulgence,
which is unworthy, vain and fit only for
the worldly minded—and the habitual practice,
on the other hand, of self-mortification, which is
painful, useless and unprofitable."

"Neither abstinence from fish or flesh,
nor going naked nor shaving the head,
nor wearing matted hair, nor dressing in
a rough garment, nor covering oneself with dirt,
nor sacrificing to Agni, will cleanse
a man who is not free from delusions."

"A middle path, O Bhikkus, avoiding
the two extremes has been discovered by
the Tathagata—a path which opens the eyes
and bestows understanding, which leads
to peace of mind, to the higher wisdom,
to full enlightenment, to Nirvana."

This is from Upanishads:
"There are two kinds of knowledge[1]
to be acquired." Says Angiras to Saunaka,
"The higher and the lower, this is what,
as tradition runs, the knower of the import
of the Vedas say."

"(By the higher knowledge) the wise realize
everywhere that which cannot be perceived
and grasped; which is without source, features,
eyes and ears; which has neither hands nor feet;

[1]Mundaka Upanishad, 1, 1-4, 6

which is eternal, multiformed, all-pervasive,
extremely subtle, and undiminishing;
and which is the source of all."

Again:
"The means for the attainment of the other world,"[1]
Says Yama (the Lord of Death) to Naciketa,
"does not become revealed to the non-discriminating man
who blunders, being befooled by the lure of wealth.
One that constantly thinks that there is only this world
and none hereafter, comes under my sway
again and again."

"Living in the midst of ignorance and
considering themselves intelligent and
enlightened, the senseless people
go round and round, following crooked courses,
just like the blind led by the blind."

This is what Lao-Tsu says of Tao,
which also means the "Way":
"The Tao which can be expressed in words[2]
is not the eternal Tao; the name which can
be uttered is not the eternal name.
Without a name it is the beginning of heaven
and earth; with a name it is the mother
of all things. Only one who is ever free
of desire can apprehend its spiritual essence;
he who is ever a slave to desire can see
no more than its outer fringe.
These two things the spiritual and the material,
though we call them by different names,
in their origin are one and the same.
This sameness is a mystery. It is the gate of all wonders."

[1]Katha Upanishad, 1, 2-5, 6
[2]Tao Te Ching, 1, 1-3A.

"Now there is possible but one way to attain[1]
Salvation for man, and his soul to gain
Life in God, and there is not one for the Jew"
Says William Law, (whose words great wisdom shew,)
"Another for a Christian and a third
Meant for a heathen," (that is where we erred)
"No; God is one and human nature one
Salvation one and the way to it one,
And that is soul's desire turned to God."
This, broadly speaking, is well in accord
With the Enlightened view of God and Soul:
The law of Evolution and its Goal,
Which from the times of fabulous Hermes found
Expression in all mystical thought profound.

This from Guru Nanak:
"He Who made the night and day,[2]
The days of the week and the seasons,
He who made the breezes blow, the waters flow.
The fires and the lower regions,
Made the earth—the temple of Law.

He Who made creatures of diverse kinds
With a multitude of names,
Made this the Law—
By thought and deed be judged forsooth,
For God is true and dispenseth truth."

This from Rig Veda:
"May Varuna with guidance straight, and[3]
Mitra lead us, he who knows,
And Aryaman in accord with Gods.
For they are dealers forth of wealth, and,
Not deluded, with their might,
Guard evermore the holy Laws.

---

[1]The Spirit of Prayer.
[2]Hymns of Guru Nanak, Trans. by Khushwant Singh.
[3]Rig Veda I.XC, Trans. by R.T.H. Griffith.

126

Shelter may they vouchsafe to us, immortal
Gods to mortal men, chasing our enemies away.
May they mark out our Paths to Biss, Indra
The Maruts, Pusan and Bhaga, the gods to be adored
Yea, Pusan, Visnu, ye who run your course,
Enrich our hymns with kine;
Bless us with all prosperity.
The winds waft sweets, the rivers pour
Sweets for the man who keeps the Law:
So may the plants be sweet for us.
Sweet be the nights and sweet the dawns,
Sweet the terrestrial atmosphere;
Sweet be our Father Heaven to us.
May the tall trees be full of sweets for us,
And full of sweets the Sun:
May our milch-kine be sweet for us.
Be Mitra gracious unto us, and Varuna and Aryaman:
Indra, Brihaspati be kind and Visnu
Of the mighty stride."

This is the Highway, now lost to our view,
To which most prophets man's attention drew;
A vital part of nature's Cosmic Scheme;
As binding as is eating, drinking, dream
And sleep or other functions of our life,
Whose knowledge must be as wide-spread and rife
As knowledge of our stern organic needs—
The primary function of religious creeds.

But since that confidence in faith is lost
Which it commanded once, to pay the cost
Of pride and prejudice and it has waned
In power and influence it had first gained,
A fresh apocalypse must help again
To make it guardian of the evolving brain.

That is why this established, ancient route,
Alone which man's evolving mind can suit,
Revealed from time to time to each great seer,
Instinctively became so very dear

And often exercised such iron hold
Upon the mind of its adherent fold:
They went to war, invited death and loss
But still the line it laid down did not cross.

Digressions from this natural Route invite
Disasters, for we challenge then the might
Of Powers that be with our extremely frail
Body and mind, most miserably to fail.

And every time our wrong assessments lead
To such a conflict, we as often breed
Insurgence, war and violence to right
The wrong we do with our myopic sight.
This is why our earth has become today
A boiling cauldron we view with dismay,
Because we underrate the Cosmic Force
That keeps the human race upon its course.

3

If smart computers, space-ships, cars and planes
Could bring maturity to human brains,
Then Romans who did once earth's treasures share
And surfeited were with luxurious ware,
Would not have bred the rot which fouled at last
Despite their glorious empire, spread so vast,
That rich society, in many a way
A match for e'en the wealthiest of our day,
And brought down to its knees a proud domain
Which of its wealth and might had grown too vain.

Inventions and discoveries, goods and wealth
Are one thing, wisdom, happiness and health
Another, and the former do not pave
The way to latter, were it so a knave,
Possessed of all the chattels of this age,
Should forthwith bloom into an honoured sage;

While we find often that excess of wealth
But seldom adds to wisdom, peace or health.

Were it so champions in sport or strength,
And prodigies in learning, in the length
And breadth of earth, would not be mostly born
In families of wealth and station shorn.

But strange to say we often see that fate
Acts otherwise to grant the rare estate
Of mental, physical or artistic prime
Without regard to status, wealth or clime.

Were it so, families that had once rolled
In wealth would always have retained their hold
On gold and rich possessions, were it left
To man to live in plenty or, bereft
Of e'en the barest needs, to sigh for crumbs
Of bread and tattered rags in reeking slums.

Were it so, then long, long before the dawn
Of modern science, with its aim to pawn
The soul to buy for flesh delight and ease,
Whence came the bloom of rare philosophies
In Greece and India which e'en now surpass
What modern wealth in this sphere could amass?
Whence came the wisdom of poor Vedic seers
Now the despondent rich inspires and cheers?

And was it chance or luck or knowledge, born
Of long experience, in the early morn
Of India's climb to pinnacles of thought
That there a wisdom dawned which often wrought
Upheavals in the thinking of the elite,
Of earth and still inspires the erudite?

Clearly it was the hard-won mellow fruit
Of labor done by those who chose the route
Of self-denial, contentment, truth and love,
Who battled with their minds and rose above

Surrendered mansions for a hermitage,
In their desire to win the enlightened stage,
Renounced their treasures, passions, wealth and all
That keep a contemplative mind in thrall.

The scholars who now to the skies extol
Their matchless talent, oft fail to recall
What made them great, what built that astral size
We lack today, and seldom emphasize
The way they lived ere they rose to be wise,
Ere they attained to that illumining light,
Millenniums after which still shines so bright.

They do not, as there is a curious twist
In modern thinking, like a shrouding mist,
Which bars the inference that, if to suit
The growth of wisdom there has been a route,
And that, apart from India, it had been
The practice in all cultures that had seen
Vicissitudes of time for ages past,
To stick to this prescription hard and fast:
That those who wisdom or self-knowledge sought
Had all to adopt their bodies and their thought
To simple living, noble thought and deeds—
The teaching too of all religious creeds—
As if in order to achieve the goal
This is the heaven-ordained path for the soul.

Were it not so, why curbing of desire,
Restraint on greed, check on ambition's fire
And e'en renouncement of the world became
Part of religious disciplines to tame
The mind—not in one land but all ov'r earth—
Where'er aspirants strove to gain in worth
And wisdom or where'er they strove to win
True knowledge of Eternal Life within.

Control of passion and restraint of lust
Could not command the confidence and trust

Of multitudes for vast millenniums,
When goods were meagre, habitations slums
And living standards so extremely poor,
That e'en the poorest now cannot endure,
If there were not some hidden purpose bound
With such a way of life, we have not found.

What does a human being need to live
A fruitful, happy life, himself to give
That sense of peace, content and battle won,
Which brings conviction—when life's day is done—
That our brief pilgrimage was not in vain
In rash pursuit of wealth or other gain,
But that some noble aim of lasting worth
Hallowed, at least in part, our stay on earth?

What does it cost to live an honest life
To play one's part above the dirty strife,
To live without pretension and display,
The safe, unenvied, sober, middle way,
Nor want nor wealth, enough one's needs to meet,
Thanking God for a debt-free balance sheet,
Sufficient food and clothing just to meet
The needs of body, keep off cold and heat,
A shelter ov'rhead modest, cosy, warm
In winter, cool in summer, breathing charm
Not of wealth, grandeur or expensive ware,
But order, cleanliness, good taste and care?

A mode of life, in short, that leaves one free,
Whate'er his honest occupation be,
From daily chores to turn a while within,
Out of the illusive web his senses spin,
And look with breathless wonder at the God
Who lives disguised in him, attired in sod,
A Ray of Life Eternal, neither born
Nor dying, e'er the same both eve and morn.

Who will believe my word when I assert
That our unnatural ways of life subvert

The mighty Plan of heaven to fashion man
Into a Hierarch in the shortest span
Of time, into a Seraph, dressed in clay,
On distant planets born to hold his sway;
A Cosmic sage whose intellectual size
Shall dwarf that of the wisest of our wise:
Many of whom, unlettered in the lore
Of Life, out of pride think there is no more
To learn, denying to themselves the prize
Of knowledge which alone can help them rise
Out of temporarl dross towards Divine,
And crowned with Cosmic Consciousness to shine.

Were it not for the tragedy involved
How droll some scholars should think we have solved
The riddle of life, when we do not know
The slightest bit towards what type we grow?
Where will the spinning earth transport the race
To land in heaven or but to freeze in space?
After aeonean spans of time to find
Herself with the same faults and cast of mind?
Or will it raise her up to attain a height,
Which still short-sighted knowledge cannot sight,
When diademed with a crest that has no peer
Terrestrial man will shine as Cosmic seer.

Fresh waves of thought now spreading o'er the earth:
Previsions of a New Age taking birth;
Instil new hopes that things will happen soon
To draw the race out of the oblivious swoon
Of rank materialism, disbelief and doubt,
That holds her in a firm grip, in and out;
And Powers Divine will usher in an age
Of new ideas and values, on the stage
Of earth to build a global brotherhood,
With new ideals of universal good,
Now flights of healthy, world-uniting thought,
To eject the poison of the infection caught
From writings which for all their learned worth
The soul of man bind firmly to the earth.

How can the wolf of war, rebellion, riot
Disorder and the horror of adroit
Guerrilla desperadoes flee our shore,
When wolf of hunger e'er is at the door
Of half the population of our earth:
Insane abundance facing frenzied dearth?
When ne'er-abating torments which exceed
The throes of war are caused by want and need?
When suckling babes in millions go to bed
Hungry, holding to mothers almost dead
With slow starvation, just before the eyes
Of those who billions spend to explore the skies,
And billions more to install the dread device,
Ordained to exact one day a dreadful price
For our infraction, pride and gross abuse
Of intellect lent for judicious use?

The path is lost and we, who, loud in praise
Of Krishna, Christ, Mohammad, Buddha raise
Resplendant monuments to exalt their name
Forget alas! to our unspeakable shame,
The very crux of faith they came to teach,
By which we swear, to others try to preach,
That all men, white or coloured, high or low,
Illumined by but one Eternal Glow
Of Life, are equal and our aim should be
To treat one kindly, as if we are he,
And be as good and helpful as we can
To cement with love all the tribe of man:
A fulcrum necessary to raise the race
To her divine rank and exalted place.

When e'en gregarious beasts which feed in flocks,
And ant-like insects from their garnered stocks
Of food, instinctively take proper care
That every member has a basic share;
Setting a mute example for mankind;
Why rational man, in this, should lag behind
And then forget that Laws, which firmly grip
Colossal worlds, must have the power to whip

Intractable forms of life, which set at naught
The irreversible Purpose for which brought
Into existence, and who try to squeeze
From others' blood their luxury and ease.

4

There are some long-lived trees with rings ingrained
In their trunks, which record the age attained.
The longest lived of them—the bristle-cone pines—
In thousands show of yearly rings the signs,
And it was reckoned from the rings one wears
That it had lived about five thousand years!

Experts now try to figure from their rings
Vicissitudes borne by these forest kings,
Climatic rigour, draught or e'en some sort
Of catastrophe these rings could distort,
Or otherwise affect the amazing tree
Which lived the whole course of our history!

Can be, like the rings on the bristlecone pine,
There may soon come to light a hidden mine
Of vital facts and figures in our brains
To show the effect of incidental chains,
Of modes of conduct, good and evil deeds,
For progeny to judge the inherited seeds.

Cryptic devices in the human brain
When once deciphered by the learned train,
May soon disclose the signs by which they can
Locate a more or less developed man,
For evolutionary forces stamp their mark,
About which scholars are still in the dark.

A most condensed account of all events,
Of all vicissitudes and accidents,
Of all experiences had and actions done
Passes in toto from the sire to son

In Pranic Spectrums, ruled by cosmic laws,
Of our heredity which are the cause.

To hold that structural patterns are the means,
In genetic fluids, chromosomes or genes,
To evince aeonean memories is to expose
A lack of depth and subtlety in those
Who trumpet loud opinions of this type
To show how hasty they are and unripe.
For Knowledge still completely lags behind
In grasping e'en the nature of the mind,
And, when the leading actor still goes masked
How do they tell these children's tales unasked?

Though oft the erudite revise their views
Yet always give the impression that the news
That figures as their last is accurate,
In dark themselves that at no distant date
The view they had believed would be the last,
Fresh data would compel them to recast.

One recent instance can help throw some light
To show how far some of their claims are right.
The hunt for man's ancestor going strong
Has just proved at least one opinion wrong,
Which might have well survived as amply proved
Had not the finger of Fate lately moved,
And close to Natal border shown a find
Of relics which allot to humankind
A stretch of prehistoric life more than
Three times the previously determined span.

This sent a shockwave through the learned ranks
And, as before, instead of earning thanks
The savants, who unearthed this tell-tale chest,
Have now to face the challenge of the rest
Of out-worn, die-hard skeptics holding fast
To hackneyed theories, now things of the past.

These fossils of a hundred thousand years
Show man with the same head, as he now wears,
With language, primitive culture and belief
In life's survival, governed by a chief,
Ceremonial burial, implements yet coarse,
With ev'n some knowledge of mettalic ores,
Adornments for the body, deep-sunk pits
To dig up hematite: all these fresh bits
Of evidence, proving it beyond dispute
That civilization dug its primal root,
About a hundred thousand years ago,
What first was thirty thousand years or so.

Apart from this discovery, one more thread
Of evidence, dug in Kenya of a head
Of man's ancestor, by the shape it wears,
Extends his span by o'er two million years,
Instead of half a million, once the last
Limit based on the Peking primate's cast
Of bones, perhaps to be revised again
Pending fresh evidence that has hidden lain.

Compare two million years with all the store
Of knowledge of the past we have before
Our eyes, which history could e'er record
Through priest, historian, poet or the bard,
And picture what upheavals in this span
Of time must have been seen and borne by man.

What lightnings, thunders, and torrential rains,
What devastating floods and hurricanes,
What cataclysmic tremors, earthquake shocks
Disrupted earth, shook oceans, scattered rocks
Split open mountains, turned hot barrens green,
Or into deserts changed what once had been
Blooming arboreal zones, installing seas
Where hilltops were, submerging shrubs and trees,
With countless creatures which there lived and thrived,
And ages on those pastures had survived.

What dread collisions with some asteroid
Engulfed whole regions, peopled tracts destroyed,
What baneful comets, deadly bolide rains
Frightful disruptions in the starry trains,
Must have occurred for helpless man to see
And suffer the horror in dumb agony!
During this awful, lengthy stretch of time,
To inch his way up the tormenting climb.

O, you ephemeral sparks, betrayed by those
Who spurning Truth the path to grandeur chose,
Do you suppose that all this glittering store
Of gadgets, goods and wealth, seen ne'er before,
Would stand for e'er the attacks of battering time
And ne'er be drowned again in mud and slime,
In our descendants on a future day
To cause a ferment in a similar way
As now the ruins of Greece cause in us,
When time has silenced all their fret and fuss.

With subterranean fires, storms on the sun,
Space accidents disaster can be done;
Volcanoes burst, large meteors can hit earth
And rock her terribly in all her girth,
When ocean waves full hundreds of feet high,
Withdrawing from some parts to leave them dry,
Can all at once submerge inhabited zones
To engulf, without e'en sparing earth and stones,
All that our proud technology has built,
And bury under mounds of mud and silt,
Leaving no trace, in any future age,
The cause of the catastrophe to guage.

Shallow is the intellect which, widely read,
Knows what destruction nature can spread,
What dread calamities at different times
Turned into wildernesses enchanting climes,
What grim events combined to bring to dust
Proud kingdoms in their might that had full trust,

137

Which still continues in the false belief
That it can win where others came to grief.

A wise aspirant to self-knowledge must
First learn to sift his consciousness from dust;
The saving truth with firm conviction hold
That soul is separate from the mortal mould
In a relative sense; for as the base
It is the mind and body, time and space.

Then take a good look at the objective side:
The world in which we all our life abide
To toil and battle hard, to pull and heave
With all our wit and strength until we leave
As void and empty-handed as we came,
Handing away our goods, wealth, power, e'en name.

And then impartially his judgment pass
For what do we exhaust ourselves to amass
In gross excess of our essential needs,
Wasting the time in feverish thought and deeds
Which, if judiciously apportioned, can
Lead to his Kingdom self-defrauding man.

A gaudy colored bubble, born to burst,
More plagued than calmed by many an itch and thirst,
He seldom ponders on the truth sublime
That endless crowds like him came in their time
And left again soon with no lasting gain,
And to the end will do the same in vain,
Making the ceaseless round of birth and death
An empty dream, a vanishing trail of breath!

And what does it avail if all through life,
Health has abounded, pleasures have been rife,
Success has, like a handmaid, always stood
Ready with fine attire, goods, drink and food;
Untold wealth, rare adventure, ready wit
Have fallen to our portion every bit,

And fame, that widely sought alluring dame,
In every quarter has made known our name,
When, like an executioner, old age grips
Our throat to dim our eye sight, silence lips,
Wither our body, cripple legs and arms,
And make a hideous scarecrow of our charms
To live dependent for the rest of life,
A tedious load on children, friends and wife,
Until in mercy death severs the knot
Which to the body links the fount of thought.

Do you think nature has this end in view,
A gloomy, dismal end, save for a few,
For this susceptible thinking tribe of man,
To die in suffering after a brief span
Of smiling youth and full-grown, radiant prime,
And be then tortured at the hands of Time?

The mere thought of such irretrievable doom
Can damp one's spirit e'en in youthful bloom,
And make age, like a haunting spectre loom
Before his mind to plunge deep into gloom.
But nature mercifully knows how to blunt
The mind to gloomy prospects just in front.

Were it not so, at least, intelligent men
Would keep the end of life before their ken
To guard against this haggard witch in time,
And make provision, in the bloom of prime,
To arrest, defer or e'en avert the doom
With self renewal for which there is room.

If such were not the case, ambitious youth
Would show in time awareness of this truth,
And not exhaust soon but conserve his strength
To spend it frugally for the whole length
Of life's short journey that too often ends
In suffering which it to the last attends.

If such were not the case then seasoned prime
Would earlier show much more regard for time,

139

Knowing it well that in a few more years
Decreptitude would storm the flesh he wears,
Leaving him ill equipped to face alone
The assault of death to strike cold flesh and bone;
And taking life in a more serious way
Would know that Death does not miss nor delay.

If such were not the case, at least the aged,
Now tottering on the verge, would be engaged
In pious acts that bring peace to the soul,
But, far from it, they not unoften roll
The other way, to nurse and nurture plans
Which all the fires of flesh ignite, like fans,
And keep on fanning e'en when laboured breath
Arrives to warn, and the eyes close in death.

Accuse not nature for it has no plan
To thrust a lingering death on rational man,
For there are methods, known to ancient seers,
Which when employed, the body slower wears;
And rich rejuvenizing hormones cure
Full many faults and ills we now endure.
This shows that strength, wit, charm and longer span
Of life, are nature's still hid gifts for man.

So human life is not, as we suppose,
To be a bed of thorns, and come to close
In the relentless hold of senescence,
That dark, confusing gloom of failing sense,
Of ceaseless vain regrets for faded prime,
And anguish at the unrecallable time
When love, adventure, travel, sport or game
Kept happy and amused the living flame,
Deprived of movement, hobby, health, e'en breath
To sink at last into engulfing death.

You are a King although you know it not,
The monarch of the Cosmos in your thought,
A sun, a star, a moon that has no peer
For what the world is worth without a seer,

You are the Eternal Flame which ne'er expires
Nor flickers nor grows dim, nor ages nor tires.
The Wonder of creation sole and whole—
Though you may not believe it—is your soul!

It is the mystery of mysteries
Which ne'er can be explained, and nev'r shall cease
For ages, if men the secret try to find,
Until exhausted they turn to the mind,
And in this mirror see what was denied
Before—the Seer and Seen identified.

Thousands of years ago, this Truth was known
To Indian sages, who the way have shown
To experience it with discipline of thought
And conduct, when a miracle is wrought
And one's Flame of awareness shines so bright
That it remains the one and only light,
In which the enigma of existence fades,
Like as the morning sun dissolves the shades
Of night, and dominates the earthly scene,
For where is darkness now that there had been?

This is the secret of perennial peace,
Which travelled far to Arabia, Rome and Greece
To China, Japan and full many lands
In time to branch out into different brands,
And now all over earth provides again
Religious comfort for the fevered brain.
This is the only prize that makes it worth
For man to endure the suffering of his birth,
To know that his ephemeral life enshrines
The Eternal Light with which creation shines.

5

Suppose it is established, in the course
Of time, that our soul is, indeed, the source,
Pervasive and eternal, hid behind
The cosmic panorama shown by mind;

And that the goal of human life decreed
By nature is to open up with speed
A higher channel of perception—now
In but a rudimentary form—to allow
The brain to catch impressions which now fall
Unheeded, shut out by the sensual wall,
Would it not be but wisdom then to assume
That our mind has to attain a richer bloom,
And to perform a more rewarding role
To manifest the glory of the soul?

The alternatives are that either man
Shall stay confined within the present span,
Extremely narrow, of his senses or
He has in him a hid potential for
The growth of yet another sense to win
Approach to eternal planes of life within,
Which by no other means our mind can reach
For walls of space and time are hard to breach.

In order, therefore, to secure access
To new dimensions of our consciousness
Our mind must needs take yet another bound
To enter realms more subtle and profound
Than those we every moment round us see
And oft think this is all that there can be.

To hold that man has now no scope to grow
A higher faculty, designed to show
The still Unseen, is first to prove untrue
Experiences, to which we have no clue,
Of prophets, mystics, sages and the rest
Some of whom proved to be the very best
Of all the hierarchy that made mankind
What she is now, rich, cultured and refined.

Most of them claimed, in unambiguous terms
Kinship with higher beings which confirms
That other avenues of knowledge can
Open new vistas to the sight of man.

Besides this, such a viewpoint would condemn
To eternal servitude the priceless gem
Of life, awareless of its own estate,
About its nature, origin, or state
After demise, and doom the immortal spark
Through·all its life to flounder in the dark,
And die in torment never sure about
Its own imperial stature and without
Knowing e'en once what it is, whence it came,
Always to admit its own defeat with shame,
Always to be pricked by the thorns of doubt,
Always perplexed what all this is about:
A ceaseless torture for a sensitive brain,
Enough to turn all pleasure into pain.

And what does it avail if pampered with
The goods of luxury one's gait is blithe,
And face in smiles, the body strong and stout,
When mind is restless, racked by ceaseless doubt,
Which gains in volume as the end draws near,
Adding to his uncertainty and fear
Of what lies hid beyond the fateful screen
That keeps him wondering what his death would mean:
Whether it would lead to an awakening soon
To another life or but to an endless swoon;
A state of fix which for intelligent brains
Can sour the joy of all temporal gains.

The wise dispensers of our weal and woe,
Whom we our present tight position owe,
Who still engaged in thousands everywhere
Are building fresh stocks of luxurious gear;
Our rulers, scholars, scientists and priests,
Who seem to act as if they deal with beasts
Who must be fed and clothed well or with ease
Have what they like to enjoy life as they please,
As if what matters is their bone and skin,
Without a thought towards the soul within.

Would not a sudden, allround change occur
In human thought if it once comes to light
That our one-sided efforts to confer
Untold amenities on flesh, though right
To some extent, indulged in to excess
React so sharply that they cause distress
In just proportion to the effort lost
In pampering body at the spirit's cost?

Can we arrest by binding them up tight
The growth of children to the natural height?
Without disastrous consequences, sure
To follow soon the ill effects to cure,
To mend the serious deformations wrought
By our outrageous act and crazy thought?

The same is true of us and all our hard
And constant efforts only done to award
A much augmented share to flesh than mind,
Which oft the latter is taxed hard to find—
And keeps it from the size it has to attain—
Cannot but meet a sharp repulse with pain.

Do you think nature which is so severe
In dealing with us, when we choose to err
And flout organic laws, would turn to milk
When our insane desire for cream and silk,
For cars and soft ways of life tends to stunt
The growth of brain and would not then the brunt
Of her explosive ire be borne by those
Their eyes to past deterrent lessons close,
And, fooled by bright but hollow logical tricks
Of depthless writers, spurn their faith with kicks?

We mark this strong resistance of the flesh
And mind, when we attempt by force to crush
The growing instinct of a child to apply
Itself to a game or hobby which we try
To keep it from, or, when grown up, it likes
To adopt a certain course, say go on hikes,

Which we debar, oft leading to revolts,
Nature's response to using locks and bolts;
Which argues that an inborn armour binds
The inherent tendencies of human minds.

How can these frantic efforts of the elite
Of our day, aimed to force our bodies tight
Into surroundings that are all against
The inherent trends of our evolving brains,
Be e'er successful and not generate soon
A strong world-wide reaction to attune
Their wrong ideas to nature's global plan
To make a cosmic-conscious seer of man.

It shows a tragic lack of knowledge in
The architects of modern life who pin
Their faith in gimmicks to improve the plight
Of people, heedless whether it is right,
And in accordance with the natural trends
In human bodies for predestined ends.

And, if they have no inkling of this fact,
And hold their faith in word but not in act,
Do they not morally owe it to those
Of whom they as friends and well wishers pose,
To solve the conflict as soon as they can
Between the faith and intellect of man?

Too much reliance on the wisdom shown
By modern intellects, whose thought has sown
The seeds that built the world we see today,
Is at the bottom of the grim array
Of adverse forces which are gathering fast
To wreck—as always they did in the past,
When bodies grew obese and minds decayed—
The rich assortments brazenly displayed
Of chattels that make human bodies soft
And cause disasters ordered from aloft.

Do not our mentors and our rulers vie
With one another for soon bringing nigh
The flowering of full many ambitious schemes
To build Utopias of their cherished dreams?
Ready with promises to ensure our weal,
Our safety, freedom and a fairer deal,
Abundance, education, business, wealth,
Amusement, pleasure, physical strength and health;
All but intent on flesh, the alluring mass
Of rosy tissue which they think is brass
In its resistance, as if unaware
That flesh its life with only soul can share!

But in their fervour no one cares the least
Whether this highly spiced material feast
Which they prepare for mankind, with the aim
To do their best for her corporeal frame,
Will also be digestible to the soul,
And help it onward to the appointed goal,
Or cause acute disorder with great pain
To make them change their way of thought amain.

Science with no thought to the soul within,
Whate'er the crests and triumphs it may win,
The moment it discards the appointed route
To take one of its choice, which does not suit
The growing stature of the evolving brain,
Must meet reverses with great loss and pain;
And this has happened since the Atlantean race
And other fabled cultures turned their face
From Truth: remote disasters which we find
As legends present in the racial mind.

This is what Krishna says:
"Whenev'r O Arjuna, there is decline[1]
Of Dharma, (Heaven-appointed Path divine),
And evil grows ascendant, then I come
Clad in a body (to wipe off the scum)."

_____

[1]Bhagwad Gita IV-7, 8

146

"For the protection of the righteous and
For the destruction of the evil brand
And to plant Dharma firmly I take birth .
From age to age (to purge sin-laden earth)."

This the Bible:
"And Moses called all Israel and said unto[1]
them . . . . When thou hast eaten and art full
then thou shalt bless the Lord thy God for
the good land which he hath given thee.

Beware that thou forget not the Lord
thy God in not keeping his commandments,
and his judgments, and his statutes,
which I command thee this day:

Lest when thou hast eaten and art full,
and hast built goodly houses,
and dwelt therein;

And when the herds and flocks multiply,
and thy silver and thy gold is multiplied,
and all that thou hast is multiplied;

Then thine heart be lifted up, and thou forget
the Lord thy God, which brought thee forth
out of the land of Egypt from the house
of bondage . . . .
And thou say in thine heart, my power
and the might of mine hand hath gotten me
this wealth . . . .

And it shall be, if thou at all forget the Lord
thy God . . . .

As the nations which the Lord destroyeth
before your face, so shall ye perish;

---

[1]Deuteronomy 8

147

because ye would not be obedient
unto the voice of the Lord your God."

This from Kena Upanishad:
"If one has realized here, then there is truth;[1]
if he has not realized here, then there is
great destruction. The wise ones, having
realized (Brahman) in all beings and,
having turned away from this world,
become immortal."

This the Quran:
"But if the truth were to follow their lusts,[2]
heavens and the earth would be corrupted
with all who in them are!—Nay, we brought
them their reminder but they from their
reminder turn aside . . . .
And, verily, thou dost call them to
a right way; but, verily, those who
believe not in the hereafter from
the way do veer.
But if we had mercy on them, and removed
the distress they have, they would persist
in their rebellion, blindly wandering on.
And we caught them with the torment,
but they did not abase themselves before
their Lord, nor did they humble themselves;
until we opened for them a door with
grievous torment, then lo! they are
in despair."

This from Hermes Trismegistus:
". . . But the Justice is ordained avenger of those[3]
sinning upon earth. For the race of men,
since mortal and consisting of evil matter,

[1]Kena Upanishad, II-5
[2]Quran XXIII, 70-80
[3]Stoboeus, Physica—134

148

. . . and especially to them occurs
the lapsing, with whom Godseeing power
is not present; over these then, and especially,
does the justice prevail, and they are
subjected to the Fate through the energies
of the generation; but to justice through
the sins in the life."

This from Buddha:
"All that we are is the result of what[1]
we have thought; it is founded on our thoughts,
it is made up of our thoughts. If a man
speaks or acts with impure thoughts,
sorrow follows him as the wheel follows
the foot of the draught animal that draws
the carriage . . . .
He who lives without passionate craving
for sensuous pleasures, his senses
well controlled, moderate in his food,
faithful and strong, him the Tempter
will certainly not over-throw, any more
than the wind throws down a rocky mountain."

This Lao-Tsu:
"When the people lack a proper sense[2]
of awe, then some awful visitation
shall descend upon them."

This from Plato:
"God who, as the old saw has it, holds[3]
in his hands beginning, end and middle
of all that is, moves through the cycle
of nature, straight to his end, and ever
at his side walks right, the Justicer of them
that foresake God's Law. He that would be happy

---

[1]Dhammapada
[2]Tao Te Ching LXXII, 174
[3]Laws IV-716

follows close in her train with lowly
and chastened mien, but whoso is lifted up
with vanity—with pride of riches or rank
or foolish conceit of youthful comeliness—
and all on fire within with wantonness,
as one that needs neither governor nor guide,
but is fitted rather to be himself a guide
to other—such a one is left alone,
forsaken of God. In his abandonment he takes
to him others like himself, and works general
confusion by his frantic career. Now to some
he seems to be some great one, but after
no long while he makes no stinted amend
to right by the sheer ruin of himself,
his house and his state."

This is exactly what has come to pass;
For heedless of the Law the leading class
Of mankind, sick with indigestion, may,
To meet the Law, on some ill-omened day,
Cause havoc, using the atrocious scourge
Of war, with dreadful agony to purge
The race of sensuous poisons which impede
The path of soul towards the glorious meed
Of self-awareness, nature's highest prize
For those who disciplined, austere and wise
Pursue the appointed route to reach the state
Of Cosmic Knowledge, writ in human Fate.

6

What some aspirants to self-knowledge seek
Are also gimmicks, some loophole or leak
In nature's rigid laws, with ease to find
A shortcut to the higher realms of mind,
To God or soul or to miraculous gifts
So that a seeker, while he idly drifts
Or lives a dissolute life at his choice
Might in the blissful sight of God rejoice.

150

This is the turn in these enlightened days
Which human thought has taken to find ways,
Methods and talismans that can ensure
For our inquietitude a lasting cure;
That like an omnipotent magic balm
Can grant us vision, mental bloom and calm,
Lift us above the storm and stress of life
To live in beatitude, immune from strife;
And this is promised to the old and young
By many a fertile pen and ready tongue!

And this is promised to the old and young
This beatific estate, the upmost rung
Of human life, the last meridian stage
Of evolution, in this reckless age
By good men, as awareless as the rest
That it will nev'r be possible to wrest
This gift sublime from nature's iron hold,
Except with methods which conduce to mould
Our brain and body to the needed pitch.
Supernal visions where our mind enrich;
Opening a higher center in the brain
Designed to explore the transcendental plane
Of life, beyond our mind and intellect
Which needs another channel to detect.

A gracious impulse in our mortal frame,
Designed to enhance the lustre of the Flame
Of consciousness, at work in all the cells
And tissues of the body in which dwells
The invisible stream of life, by slow degrees,
Resplendent, with the humming sound of bees,
Moulds all our visceral organs and the brain
A new dimension for our mind to gain.

How can a deep ingrained electric spark,
About which knowledge is still in the dark;
The spark of life in us, we ne'er can scan
Be made subservient to the will of man?

And they who claim that this can come to pass
And those believing them reveal such crass
And blinding ignorance that they, it seems,
More than reality rely on dreams.

How an almighty Power which, in the womb,
Fashions the embryo, buried in a tomb
Beyond our reach, to which we owe our all,
By which we live, by which we rise or fall,
Our dear life, still a mystery to us,
Can we control or like a chicken truss,
When we ourselves obedient to her string,
Till death like puppets move, act, dance and sing.

A marvelous mechanism, still unknown
To knowledge, with a saga of its own,
Reaching to prehistoric times, directs
A most amazing process which effects
Mutations in the body and the brain,
With such intelligence in a regular chain
That beats the marvel of embryonic growth
In its complexity and wonder both.

Incredible that some seekers of today,
And e'en those who believe they know the way,
Should e'er suppose they can direct the course
Of a mighty Cosmic Energy—the source
Of all existence, thought, desire and will—
With backdoor methods or conjuring skill,
With Mantras, charms, spells or professional aid;
As if the guidelines and conditions laid
By heaven can be so lightly set aside;
O, what a cloud of ignorance and pride!

The brain and nervous system have to reach
The right formation for the mind to breach
The wall of senses to land in a new
And rich world of awareness, there to view
With rapture what it ne'er can glimpse before:
The soul, a Prince now on his native shore.

The aim of all religious striving done,
Of discipline imposed or merit won,
Observance, worship, prayer, virtuous deed,
Enjoined by every healthy faith and creed,
Is but to stimulate to greater speed
This chaste device, and to pay greater heed
Towards our mode of life, behaviour, thought
And act until a wondrous change is wrought,
And what we thought was happening all around,
Outside and distant from us, is now found
To be the inside drama of a vast,
Unbounded "I" with the world as its cast.

This is what Bhagwad Gita says:
"Passion, anger and greed, these constitute[1]
the triple gate of hell leading to
the damnation of the soul. Therefore
one should shake off all these three.

A man released from these three gates to hell,
Arjuna, works his own salvation and
thereby reaches the highest goal.
He, who, having cast aside the injunctions
of the scriptures, acts according to
his own sweet will, attains nor perfection,
nor the highest goal, nor even happiness."

This from Christ:
"And he said unto them, take heed,
and beware of covetousness: for a man's life
consisteth not in the abundance of
the things which he possesseth . . . .
And seek ye not what ye shall eat, or
what ye shall drink, neither be ye
of doubtful mind. For all these things do
the nations of the world seek after: and
your Father knoweth that ye have need

[1]Bhagwad Gita, XVI, 21, 22, 23.

153

of these things. But rather seek ye[1]
the Kingdom of God; and all these things
shall be added unto you. Fear not
little flocks; for it is your Father's
good pleasure to give you the Kingdom."

This from Adi Granth:
"Close thou the nine doors of the body,[2]
(the nine apertures, two eyes, two ears, etc.)
and make thou still thy wandering mind,
then enter thy abode through the Tenth Door,
(the Third Eye or the Supersensory channel)
Where day and night one hears the Cosmic Sound,
audible only through the grace of the Guru."

This from Rumi:
"While sitting at ease, the mystic by a secret Path
(the Third Eye or the Tenth Door)
visits hundreds of worlds."

Because of this immortal seed of Truth
In all the great religions of mankind,
Stressing the ways of life that render smooth
Organic changes which expand the mind,
They won esteem and power and could survive
So long, commanded such devoted care
That after ages they are still alive,
And still for hungry souls serve healthy fare.

How can a hundred powerful lights disclose
To one the shape of his own eye or nose,
So how can random efforts made to know
The Knower e'er succeed, e'en if we grow
The finest crop of instruments to aid

[1]Luke 12, 15, 29, 30, 31, 32.
[2]Adi Granth, p. 124.

Our senses which themselves conceal and shade
What we are searching for—the observing mind,
Designed to look in front and not behind
Into itself, unless we change its mould,
Then only it reveals its wealth untold.

Our life is ended watching day by day
With rapt attention an illusive play,
In which as actors and spectators we
Are ne'er free from the cloud of mystery,
And ne'er can lend a meaning to the show,
Howe'er in secular knowledge we may grow,
And to the ending breath live always lost
In speculations which great effort cost;
But e'en with all the labour ne'er can cleave
The illusive web which but our senses weave.

Encircled by our intellect and mind,
We ne'er the versatile illusionist find;
Unless transformed by yet another birth
We extend the measure of our mental girth,
When Lo, the curtains part to expose the soul,
Caught in the act, playing a double role,
Both as the mystified observer "I,"
And the Magician whose tricks grasp defy.

O, Thou Almighty Power that as our soul
And as the cosmos playest every role,
Dost each and every action that is done
By cosmic multitudes and every one
Of us, out of compassion and Thy Grace,
Grant us protection and the strength to face
The battle of life which Thou has decreed
With truth and honesty in thought and deed.

Let every one of us donate his mite
To serve the race, to uplift it and unite;
Until the august Purpose Thou hast willed
Of its existence nobly is fulfilled;
And wisdom now prevails to save from Wrath
Our inadvertent strayings from the Path,

In ignorance of Thy inviolate Law
Thou hast ordained to Thee mankind to draw.

May peace descend into all troubled hearts
And Right guide the performance of our parts;
May nature act and heavenly bodies shine
To be auspicious to us and benign.
In Thy unbounded territory O God,
Let us Thy creatures, clinging to this clod
Of earth, one out of countless earths in space,
Awareless of Thy might, out of Thy grace,
Be saved from harm in elemental strife
In which Thy Grace alone now saves our life.

Give us our daily bread, destroy our pride,
So that we all in peace and joy abide,
Let hearts unite to share in want and grief,
To help the poor, to ailing bring relief,
Quench fires of hate and quell the blight of dearth
To install a golden era on the earth.

The End.